NOW THAT YOU ARE A LEADER

A Transitional Adaptive Guide for

NEWCOMERS TO THE WORLD OF LEADERSHIP

BY

DR. PAULA A. PRICE, PHD

Created 2014 ©, Revised 2019 ©
Dr. Paula A. Price, PhD
All Rights Reserved

Created 2014 ©, Revised 2019 ©
Dr. Paula A. Price, PhD
All Rights Reserved

TABLE OF CONTENTS

CHAPTER 1 7
Leadership Development Training 7
Usable Takeaways: 12
CHAPTER 2 14
Your Leadership Position's R.O.A.D.W.A.Y 16
CHAPTER 3 17
Activating Your Consciousness Shifting Processes 17
Working Through Your Leadership Adjustment Period 18
Summarizing Thought Pointers So Far 20
My Proposed Leadership Strengtheners, Definers, and Refiners 21
Acting on What You Read 22
Proceeding to Initiate or Perform What You Read 23
CHAPTER 4 24
Familiarizing Yourself with Leadership's Major Elements 24
Thinking It Through, Working It Out, Assimilating It 27
CHAPTER 5 29
Promotion Creates a New Life Form in a World 30
Do Your Home Work Before Promotion 31
Consider the Situation This Way 32
First Responses to Your Rise 33
Ministry's New Day 34
How We Got Here & God's Response 34
CHAPTER 6 36
Leadership Appointer Wisdom 36
God's Leadership Proving, Pruning, Appointment Methods 36
CHAPTER 7 40
Your Thinkers 40
The Actors 42

Created 2014 ©, Revised 2019 ©
Dr. Paula A. Price, PhD
All Rights Reserved

Actions, Actionizers, and Actionables Inspired By Your Reading 42
The Transmitters 44
Upbuilding and Broadening 46

CHAPTER 8 .... **49**
The Constructors and Expanders 49

CHAPTER 9 .... **52**
Who Can and Should Count on Your Leadership 52
Twelve Ways You Must Prime Your Family for Your Leaderhship 53
Anticipate and Prepare 56
Family and Friends Love Driven Backlash 60

CHAPTER 10 .... **62**
The Self-Celebratory and Self- Deprecating Leaders 62
The Self-Deprecating Leader 64

CHAPTER 11 .... **67**
Initial Adversity Often Has a Short Shelf Life 67
Laying the Ax to the Root 67
A Point of Clarification 70

CHAPTER 12 .... **73**
It's In You to Pull It Out; Don't Throw It Away 73
Rediscovering and Powering Your Leadership Qualifications 75
Leadership is So Much More Than Paperwork 76
Time to Stop Reading and Start Acting 78
THEORY TO PRACTICE KNOWLEDGE TRANSFERENCE MATRIX 78

CHAPTER 13 .... **80**
Functioning in Your New Leadership Position 80
Reasons Leadership Promotion Changes Must Be 81
Additional Reading Exercise 83
Working on Your Spiritual Wisdom and Intelligence 83
Learn and Lead Exercise 85

Inducting the Above as an Incoming Leaders 85
CHAPTER 14 .... **86**
Classic Expectations Required of Your Leadership 86
New Leader Shocks & Wake Ups 88
CHAPTER 15 .... **91**
The Human Capital 'C' Suite 91
The Wisdom Pack Consists of: 92
Follow Up Reinforcement 93
Wisdom Pack Observations Task 93
Awakened Latent Leadership Talents Affirm Destiny 94
Leaders are More Than Mechanics 95
CHAPTER 16 .... **99**
Business & Entrepreneurship Equal Covenant 99
Succumbing to Requisite Leadership Changes 100
Be Different to Become Exceptional 101
The Currency of Positivity 102
New Leader Wake Up Stunners 105
Earning Trust and Sustaining It 108
Guardianship Guidance 109
CHAPTER 17 .... **111**
Personal Leader Self-Regulation Advice 111
About Adaptive Changes 113
New Leader Inward Checkups 114
Empowering & Authorizing Your Leaders Responsibly 119
CHAPTER 18 .... **121**
Making Right Selection Decisions 121
INDEX 130

Created 2014 ©, Revised 2019 ©
Dr. Paula A. Price, PhD
All Rights Reserved

CHAPTER 1
LEADERSHIP DEVELOPMENT TRAINING

This is an immersive training process that melds readers' interaction with its discussions and instruction. It does so by tasking them with educative regimens that call upon them to use what they learn promptly. Material is segmented for trainees to engage with pivotal portions of the content. The final effect is synthesized enhancement of new leaders' abilities that aid their orientation and persuades them of the unmitigable changes they must make to succeed in their promotions. Effectively, the treatments in this process blend the cognitive and affective domains so they infuse learners with practicalities of prudent leadership. As an orientation guide, this book is useful as a syllabus, tutorial, and worktext and augments textbooks,  audio-video instruction, and essential pragmatic reinforcement. Instruction and guidance map and trace key knowledge new leaders need to guard and steer their early days of leadership down well-worn, tried and proven pathways. Of the numerous features and elements that distinguish this work from others of its kind is the repeated emphases placed on metrics.

Instructants learn how important it is to measure performance and the attributes that provide benchmarks for qualitative service. With this is the broad range of learner comprehensions that fill in gaps that may trip new leaders up down the line. Also, there are the indications that lay the groundwork for creating assessable criteria to gauge learner and trainee subject matter intake and output. Particularly effective for seminars, workshops, modules, and similar knowledge cultivation and retention venues, "Now That You are a Leader" is adaptable. It can be modified to fit any other setting where new leaders must be orientated to their new world. The intelligent approach articulates apparent and nuance areas and issues that cannot be easily taught or stressed during the formal readiness process. This study guide more suited to mentorship or similar arrangement that a systematic course. Although, it can be adjusted to augment such learning teaching environments.

TUTORIAL OVERVIEW

In the way of a summary, this tutorial's topic speaks to those just entering the world of leadership, regardless of organization or sphere. It also speaks to those interested in restarting their leadership perspectives and practices to conform them to more effective approaches. Those approaches known to enhance leaders' service and mentalities. In addition, it at times contradicts the notion that leadership is little more than a variation of promotee's everyday life. A little more responsibility, a bit more visibility, and perhaps some prestige depending upon the position is pretty much all there is to it. This training dispels such myths by introducing entrant leaders to the realities that await them as and newcomer to the world of leadership. Most notably is the reality that leadership imposes changes that alter the way the new leader lives, works, relates and interacts with the old and the new world. The leadership scape is addressed in detail, pointing out the differences that impose change.

1. SUPPLEMENT GUIDES & GAINS

The guides and gains to be derived from this tutorial include:

a) Information on what entering leadership entails expects you to identify what does and does not make for leadership as its sphere has instituted and maintains it.

b) A collection of changes your promotion demand of you is looking for statements and ideas that indicate the realization of leaders' nonnegotiable changes to adapt to their new world.

c) How others are likely to view your promotion seeks new leaders' awareness of the inevitable mixed reactions to their promotion to leadership.

d) Winning over followers and workers scans for signs of inherent leadership influences that suggest newcomer to leadership has the potential to attract, mobilize, and supervise those they lead with dignity and elegance.

e) Examining yourself as a leader gleaning for methods and techniques leader personally developed over the years to self-check as a person and as a professional.

f) What to do with opposition to your elevation examines leaders' emotional honesty and its capacity to self-confront and accurately assess their emotions, motivations, habits, conduct, and behaviors for integrity, ethicalness, and objectivity.

g) How to prepare family members for your new position questions leaders' sense of duty to those most affected by promotion to leadership and the ways friends and family are prepared and reconciled to the global changes to alter their life.

h) Typical leadership roles, duties, and responsibilities queries and evaluates new leaders' sense of duty, cultivation of best practices as a leader, and conscientiousness in observing as well as executing these aspects of their position.

i) Special advice to new leaders judges hearing and heeding skills, adaptability actions, acceptance of counsel and correction, and capability to behave responsibly when these occur in the course of discharging the position.

2. SUPPLEMENT INTERACTIONS:

To get the most out of this tutorial's subject matter, participants should treat its wisdom as a fundamental adaptation to their new position's effectiveness, and the professional consciousness that assures their success in it. *Observable in participants initial and progressive acceptance of tutorial handling of its subject matter, determined by comments, questions and other responses to the material.*

3. **SUPPLEMENT GOAL:**

To introduce and alert newcomers to any type and spectrum of leadership to its world, exposing and separating its myths from reality. *Attainable by little or no dispute or resistance to the realities that await newcomers to the world of leadership.*

4. **SUPPLEMENT RATIONALE:**

The best reason for engaging in this subject's supplements is proper initiation to the world of leadership. *Noticeable by participant all-inclusive shift in perspectives and expectation of leadership role from viewing it as incidental to realizing and embracing its adaptabilities for quality performance.*

5. **SUPPLEMENT OBJECTIVES:**

The most practical steps to take to engage in this tutorial's sessions and engage in its actions. The best steps to take are:

a. Approach material with a few preconceptions or contentions as possible. Bring curiosity that seeks clarification instead.
   - Do this by choosing to relax your prior knowledge and beliefs and redirecting your thoughts to what is to come. Prepare questions to ask and possible answers instead.
b. Process articles information as objectively as possible, meaning as if you are hearing even familiar things for the first time.
   - Do this by withholding judgments and conclusions until you have taken time to compare and associate article statements with what your new leadership position holds for you.
c. Pay attention to syllabus requirement, connect them to what article says and to what your new leadership position holds in store for you.
   - Do this by studying the syllabus, concentrating on its contents, and relating what you read to what it contains in order to receive wisdom and development it outlines.
d. Use what you learn promptly to test your knowledge.
   - Do this by following instructions, completing learning and enrichment tasks and assessing yourself based on what syllabus outlines and material says.

6. **SUPPLEMENT OBSERVABLE OUTCOMES:**

Identifying rewards of engaging with this unit anticipate its use according to readings and discussions. It is expected that participants upon employing or implementing material read and studied can reap the following gains as a reward for meticulously engaging in these supplements:

   a) A greater and soberer perception of leadership in general and insight into your particular leadership spectrum and the role you are to fill.
      - Detected in changed attitudes, expectations and utilization of material.
   b) Planned initiatives to set patterns, based on acquaintance with true leadership duties and responsibilities, used as a platform for your leadership's best practices.

- Identified in way article material is used to alter entry approaches to leadership guided by specific insights being applied to early leadership decisions and actions.

c) Ways and means of adopting and thereby adapting entry to leadership consciousness typical of new leaders to what ultimately becomes reality affined[1] leadership that prudently engages in proven practices.
- Implemented by thoroughly familiarizing oneself with article recommendations and evaluating one's entrance to leadership mentality, assessments, and assumptions for correlation or conflict with effective and productive leadership criteria and matrices.

USABLE TAKEAWAYS:

Tips for fast use of tutorial material[2].

1. Takeaway knowledge: Integration of actionable truth about the world of leadership.
2. Takeaway knowhow: Recognition of new leadership factors that alter newcomer's life.
3. Takeaway ability: Devising ways of managing new leader upsets and adjustments.
4. Takeaway benefit: Advantageously justifying not buying into "leadership won't change me." assertion that misdirects and details many new leaders.
5. Takeaway capacity: Utilizing material to more readily and repeatedly adapt to the realities and requisites of leadership quickly and solidly.
6. Takeaway competency: Gradually demonstrating acclimation to leadership position's demands and better performance of its duties.

7. **SUPPLEMENT VOCABULARY:** Lists valuable words to know for assessing yourself as a leader[3].

Here are some relevant leadership words you should know and apply throughout this tutorial:

Supplement	Actionable	Actionizes	Capacity	Competency
Observable	Change	Assessment	Public	Private
Leadership	Experience	Loyalty	Change	Organization

---

[1] Joined in connection, treated or functioning in close relationship.
[2] Use takeaways as possible roleplays, scenarios, simulation exercises that draw article subject matter into the tutorial praxes.
[3] Vocabulary terms can be assigned as applied research project to forge or strengthen participants' grasp and use of article terminologies and leadership nomenclature. Goes to cultivation or transformation of participant's inner leader or inbuilding of the leader within and without.

Appointment	Promotion	Elevation	Function	Tasks
Assignments	Manage, Manageable	Expectations	Operations	Business
Practices	Weight of Responsibility	Duties	Actions	Traits
Orientation	Expertise	Capability	Capacity	Competency
Proficiency	Adaptation	Adoption	Conformance	Compliance

8. **SUPPLEMENT SCRIPTURE PREMISES:**

    These are the main Bible references tutorial uses to provide the wisest gains from this tutorial:
    - Scripture Reference 1: Matthew 25:14-30
    - Scripture Reference 2: 1 Corinthians 4:2
    - Scripture Reference 3: 2 Corinthians 8:12
    - Scripture Reference 1: Luke 19:12-27
    - Scripture Reference 1: Matthew 25:14-30

CHAPTER 2

NOW THAT YOU ARE A LEADER

A Step by Step Learning and Adaptation System

The topic you are about to cover is but a small part of Dr. Paula Price's "Welcome to the World Leadership" Orientation Program. Insofar as the orientation part goes, this instrument is to aid your enactment of the six **A**'s that settle you into your new or advanced leadership position. The six **A**'s are:

- ✪ Absorption — Take it in so it permeates entire your leadership faculties.
- ✪ Adoption — Command the material's wisdom to blend with your leadership makeup.
- ✪ Adaptation — Instruct your mind, will, and emotions to adjust to what your new role demands.
- ✪ Assimilation — Make all you read and learn an integral part of your leadership inventory and aids.
- ✪ Acculturation — Synthesize your upgraded leadership virtues and values with your new world.

✪ Application — Multiplex use of material to transformatively for ROADWAY of your new position.

The Acronym R.O.A.D.W.A.Y. Stands for:

✪	Responsibilities	Official[4] actions and initiatives that answer and resolve issues and conflicts.
✪	Obligations	Carrying out and complying with legal, moral and ethical demands associated with being put into the office of a legitimate entity.
✪	Accountability	Answerability to higher authorities as an official appointee charged with executivity, administration, problem solutioning and similar actions reliant upon professionality, competence, and capability.
✪	Duties	Obligatory undertakings tied to official service to perform tasks, functions, and related works that see to the entity's or offices smooth operations.
✪	Work	Effort exerts in the course of employment, vocation (calling) or occupation of an office to prevent, avert, address and settle issues or produce as an appointed official.
✪	Attention	Diligent proactive, and reactive actions that handle proceedings, control behaviors, plan; oversee deeds and engage techniques and practices that carry on office appointed services.
✪	Yokes	The typically disdained reality of being locked into the functions, duties, and obligations of an office and those that take part in its charges and operations.

---

[4] In office; Delegated functions and tasks related to being appointed to official service.

Your Leadership Position's R.O.A.D.W.A.Y.

For those just entering or moving up in leadership the program intends to inform you of true leadership duties, responsibilities and demands. The aim is to direct or redirect your previous notions of what leadership is and involves to what really happens when you step into its spheres and dimensions. This handout is an interactive tool to guide your reading and absorption of the material. Every so often, you will be asked to suspend your reading an perform a comprehension task.

Distressed human existences may call for you to pull back on your strengths and resolves. However, when it comes to building and sustaining institutions and agencies that enable and support it, you will find you need a strong hand, fierce resolve, and a steely will to sustain and secure your organization. Or, yourself in your new leadership position. The reason helping others as groups and not individuals relies on dealing with diverse supporters, overseers, funders, and operators. These associates are intricately attached to what your organization exists to do, and they are <u>not</u> sufferers but providers. They are businesspeople, aiders, securers who do not need to be coddled so to speak. Their contributions and donations assist your agency's intervention.

Special Note for Ministerial and Social Service Leaders

If you are entering ministerial or social service leadership, be aware that your deep-rooted sense of humanitarianism can drastically in many cases misconstrue your approaches and initiatives. Frequently, those entering leadership tend to let the endless suffering and problematic constants of this domain overly soften and cloud your perceptions and leadership judgments. Mercy and indulgence can be excessive and dispense disproportionate rules and regimens used to help the distressed get back on their feet, or in pursuit of life success. Doing so lowers the quality of service given and thereby greatly alter your leader strengths. The reason for this is how new entrants humanity's care and rescue spheres do so conditioned to think aiding the suffering requires blind emotions to express tenderness. Much of society believes helping effectively hinges on tempering the normal leadership mindset so as not to add to recipients' burdens. Often this belief and its approaches turn out to be counterproductive. Interacting with such populations may require tender approaches in one on one contacts, but the background structure that sees to organization's or agency's success does not.

So, view and treat them as cooperators, collaborators, advisory partners you count on to succeed in your new role; whether it is focusing on leadership in your organization or leadership of the populations it services. Whichever the case, you should know and prime yourself to change where necessary for the mutual benefit of all concerned, not just your own benefit or the accolades of those you leave behind.

CHAPTER 3

INITIALIZING YOUR LEADERSHIP CONSCIOUSNESS

New leader readiness starts with the mind, as do all beginner undertakings. This guide is to help you do what must be done first, which is take on the mind of the world you are entering. While culture is usually used in place of the world, for the purposes of this book, the word fits best because it encompasses cultures of all sorts. The world of leadership is more than a culture, it is a domain where leadership is engrossed in more than preferences and trends, beliefs and values, ideals and ideologies. This world teems with these and in fact emits them and then takes control of shaping a rendering them effective. Following are a few thoughts and applications to assist you in doing just that; taking on the mind of a world and not merely adorning your life with culture. Although, you thorough assimilation to this domain includes acculturation and acclimation to its primitivity and epitomized practicalities.

Immediate Reading Effects:

First.	
Second.	
Third.	

Activating Your Consciousness Shifting Processes

Accepting a leadership position does not automatically or immediately transfer to your mind or brain. The mind's conveyance of your promotion to the brain moves slowly as thoughts, despite internal and external events that compel them to do so. Your feelers must become thinkers, your sensors, conductors if you are to blast typical confusion over your advancement and turn chaos into competence. To explain, your genetic makeup may have gotten your potential recognized, but your intelligence transmitters take some time to shift from acknowledgment to assistance. That means they know something happened that places unfamiliar demands upon them, they must figure out what took place and their role in it. The disparity between the two is your day to day contact with your new post and its environment. In a word, this is called experience. Living your new life in your new world is the only way to etch and encode the parts of you that must draw your heart's wisdom into your mind for your brain to process and instruct your outer self. To get a glimpse of what is involved in all this, complete the following activity. To trigger the realizations that shape your new leader adaptations, take time to consider what you just read and how it affects your present mindsets on leadership. Contemplate your reactions and your reasons for them. Afterward, complete the following activities to work through your emotional mind on the material covered so far. Approach each section and its contents in the assigned order. Then perform or follow up what you produce with relevant reinforcement exercises. Map emotional and mental path you deem to be most advantageous to you, and other new leaders. Systematize how best to embark upon that path to settle into and manage your new position. By the time you complete the exercise, you will be better equipped to process additional thought exercises discussed in the next section.

Working Through Your Leadership Adjustment Period

Leadership has plenty of mysteries to be explored and solved. The most consequential of them is the leader's thoughts, and how they fit or conflict with its needs and norms. It hardly seems necessary to explain thinking and thoughts. Irrespective of what you know or do not know about them, thoughts' worth and dynamics are universally known and relied on throughout the world. From concepts and philosophy to teaching and learning, to creation and innovation, thoughts and thinking make up the thoroughfares to them all. People think nonstop, and what they say or otherwise publish from their mind comprises and disclose their thoughts. Thoughts are not only ideas; their place of origin says they have feelings built into their intellect. Thoughts corral, capture, and compose ideas and impressions, beliefs and sentiments; desires and determination. As ideators and imagers, thoughts paint pictures, pictures that characterize and articulate what leaders harbor or host within their soul's This statement is why people are always concerned or impressed by the 'soul' of a thing. It is perceived as the reservoir of what is inside and likely to come out of a person in various situations or provocations. Soul exploration and assessment are common but to date has proven to be quite difficult with the tools and instruments used to examine the soul tending to be intermittently reliable. Yet, the severe pressures put upon leaders say such efforts, ought to be stepped up. There remains strong indication that viable means of predicting and gauging potential leaders' compatibility and competence, before they are appointed and installed in service, is imperative. For you who are already thrust into the world of leadership, this counsel is worthwhile. Reading this material gives you a clue to what strengthens and weakens a leader and the critical factors that settle or unsettle newcomers to the world of leadership. Seeing as this guide is an interactive immersive tool, get used to the idea of internally and mentally applying it to your new life as a leader by responding to the following.

I will psychologically process what I read so far by:

a) _____.
b) _____.
c) _____.

The methods I will use to adopt the following to my leadership role start with:

Step I. _____.
Step II. _____.
Step III. _____.

The three main ways I will put forth the following efforts to increase my adaptability to this wisdom.

Step I. _____.
Step II. _____.
Step III. _____.

Summarizing Thought Pointers So Far

Basically, the foregoing sums up thoughts, their effects, intents, and mode of conveyance. As a new leader, you learn quickly your thoughts are always at issue. They emerge as major characters in all you do. If you are outspoken and talkative, your thoughts are ever on display for others to criticize or exploit. Here is why. Nontalkative leaders are considered to be sober-minded, patients, and safe. It is assumed they are strong guardians over their own thoughts and thus seen as confidantes, and so potential keepers of others' secrets. When it comes to their leaders and the persona of their, leadership, discretion and circumspection are cherishable and to be reciprocated with trust. Bear this in mind. The point is, no matter where you are on the leadership scale, what you think, how and why you think it will be scrutinized. Of the endless reasons for this truth is people need leaders to be thinkers because thoughtful leaders suggest balance and prudence. Leaders that think put people and their appointers at ease. Thoughtfulness implies restrained impulsiveness, plotted courses, and insightful stratagems. Such factors sometimes bring your thoughts into question, at other times, they are challenged. On occasion, your thoughts will be admired and if found credible, reiterated in numerous ways.

All thoughts are judged and weighted by the words and actions that broadcast them. Meaning by this, your verbal and nonverbal thoughts are constantly surveyed and, in some instances, surveilled for their relevance and merit. Yours as a new leader will be no different. These justifications and many others should move you to examine your thoughts and polish your critical thinking. The two have to become perpetual priorities in your leadership orientation processes, and thereafter. Guided by what was just said, spend some time isolating its high points and how to make them strengtheners your new leadership role. Identify significant comprehensions you could plow to nurture within yourself, right perceptions of what you just learned and will build upon throughout your leadership acclimation period. Mentally form and fit the statements below in your mind to define and refine what best suits or serves you as a leader.

My Proposed Leadership Strengtheners, Definers, and Refiners

1. Your new leader transition guide informs you of the imperatives and operatives the world of leadership subsists on, outlining its duties and responsibilities and tried and proven, or established policies and procedures diffusible to promotees such as yourself.

2. Your new leader transition guide expedites your familiarity with the leadership's commonalities and diversities, so you benefit your promoters and your subordinates quickly and definitively.

3. Your new leader transition guide covers many of the situations and incidents likely to arise as you carry out your duties.

4. Your new leader transition guide describes what leadership in action looks like and overviews some of its most efficacious procedures, performance criteria, and standards. Efficacious being the operative word in this statement.

5. Your new leader transition guide is an indispensable document for those new to leadership's world. It steers and moderates your handling of its expectations, reactions, and adaptions efficiently and temperately to accelerate your growth and conversion process.

6. In no way is this guide to be construed as a leadership offer or as a credentialer of such service. Studying this material does guarantee you any position simply on the ground of possessing or learning leadership from it alone.

7. Your new leader transition guide intends to equip and arm you with what you need to function in your leadership post capably discharging its duties well.

8. Your new leader transition guide holds vital keys to learning and complying with your promoting organization's standards, service, performance and behavior guidelines.

9. Draft a discussion with two other colleagues that justifies an organization using the wisdom contained in your new leader transition guide to uniformly address its leadership issues.

10. Describe how would erase the traditional notion that a leader's service is to be rendered exclusively at the leader's leisure, discretion, availability or convenience.

11. Draft a policy that resembles your new leader transition guide's qualifiable Readiness Placement Program for serious offers of appointment.

Acting on What You Read

Leadership is action and enacting. Your promotion assumes your ability to act readily in the capacity you are appointed to serve. Remember this, inactive leadership is not leading at all. Passivity is an antagonist to genuine leadership and carries sabotaging overtones that breed and multiply until it is sturdy enough to overthrow or deteriorate some aspect of the work. Bearing this in mind, show from the statements below how a supervisor, leader, or staff trainer demonstrates the following actions when they serve and lead. Conclude with how new leaders can go about setting standard criteria for assuring knowledge and performance in their leadership future. Responses to the following gauge your incoming views and perspectives. As you go through the program, these should change, and you should be able to say how leadership changes in you took place and what they accomplished in and may well accomplish in other new leaders. This is a pre-immersion exercise. Complete and save your responses for after the program when you can compare the differences and developments the tutorial made in you.

1. Illustrate in your own way how your new leader guide contents clarify new and existing leaders position responsibilities.

2. Propose how you would convince a newly credentialed leader of the importance of attending your leadership position's prescribed number of in-service training classes and clinics.

3. Prepare a 5-minute talk on how your new leader transition guide can be regarded as a guide to newly appointed leaders' decisions.

4. Show how a document such as this one effectively shapes incoming leaders' actions, plans, and proposals.

5. In view of modern populations' embedded resistance to rules and regulations, depict how you as a leader would substantiate and validate such mandatums' value in fulfilling organization's new leader orientation hours for their ongoing credentialing.

6. What type of answer can a new leader draft justify the premise that appointed leaders' are responsible for inquiring about their positions' in-service professional development and enroll in them on their own?

7. Develop an innovative way to enact and enforce officially appointed leaders' continually fulfilling and meeting readiness requirements for their positions.

8. Articulate cogently why and how your new leader transition guide is essential to discharge the duties and responsibilities of an appointment to leadership.

9. Compose a list of questions about codes of behavior, conduct, service, and actions you believe to be relevant to your new post. Note the ones that affect you the most.

10. Show the best ways to respond to detrimental issues and resolve organization conflicts as you would do so today, somewhat influenced by what you read so far in your new leader transition guide.

Proceeding to Initiate or Perform What You Read

The following actions are meant to enable you to sort through your present thoughts and intentions on the material you just read. Their value is your equipment for processing information responsibly. They are phrased to help your project and anticipate new leader issues outcomes in advance and intelligently plan how you would react or respond to different scenarios that await you as a new leader. To these ends, you are asked to create relevant scenarios or other responses for each of the following that may be used for by new and experienced leaders.

CHAPTER 4
FAMILIARIZING YOURSELF WITH LEADERSHIP'S MAJOR ELEMENTS

In a later section, you come across a statement that says leadership is more than paperwork. Many new leaders enter their positions with rosy-eyed notions that leadership is front lining, conspicuously standing out front to be seen and admired. Others think it is being buried under paperwork, which some used to dodge the more public demands of their post. More feel that leadership is whatever they imagined it would be when they got the opportunity to lead. There are those that feel leadership exempts them from mundanity, and boring belittling tasks they always hated doing. And, some just want to be recognized as significant with no idea or consciousness of what being a leader entail. They just want to start feeling like somebody in the world and see taking leadership posts as a quick and easy way to do so. This why many people enter the ministry. For more than a few, the last thing on their mind is service, sacrificing, suffering, and solutioning.

As you can see, judging leadership from the outside only and deciding to become a part of its world has many misleading ambitions. While some are noble, quite a number of them are errant. Image Inspired Admirations make regretful reasons for seeking to be a leader. Such motivations create a contradictory mix of deluded heart desires and leadership actualities. What leaders really do and experience is hidden beneath its mystique: the often unfathomable rigors and regimens that are so expansive and diverse those doing the job can hardly isolate and explain them. The word mystique because it describes leadership's charismatic inscrutables. Enigmatic treatment of matters and concerns most people never notice and the remainder of them could care less about. For example, leadership is a mystery, not only because of its hefty confidentiality codes but also due to the indecipherable ways and means of peculiarly fixing things and people on others' behalf. Leadership is representative, meaning it is a personal assumption of another's responsibility for reasons that go beyond remuneration. Because so many leaders do the job well, they make it look easy. But what is that job really? Let's take a moment to look at some of leadership's functions and dutifulness.

1. **Thinker's Lab:** The processes and deliberations that call for your deep and provocative thoughts on matters that may have bypassed your cognition in the past. Creates an environment to answer, resolve, proposition, or solutionize them as a leader.

2. **Action Items:** The dynamic mix of leadership tasks and praxes (acts) you will be delegated relative to why you were made a leader and what is expected of you as a newly appointed one.

3. **Office Tools:** The skillsets, faculties, techniques, and functions that facilitate your ability to fulfill your appointment as a newly entrusted leader.

4. **Responsibilities:** The liabilities and accountabilities integral to you being designated to leadership, and the scope of comprehensive services attached to your appointed position. Extends to what you are chosen to perform in the fulfillment of your duties.

5. **Duties:** Somewhat like responsibilities[5], these are the obligations, requirements, standards, and criteria that make you answerable to your appointers and their reason for choosing you. That answerability includes why you are being engaged in their service and granted their authority as an agent or similar title.

6. **Leadership**: The sphere of oversight, managerial, or supervisor that selects you and engages your abilities to get your tending to your appointing entity' business and guiding its human resources via the myriad of processes that see to its sustenance and fundamental success.

---

[5] With the distinction being acts that respond to and functions that are due those who placed you in your leadership position.

7. **Governance**: Enactment and enforcement areas of your leadership where you uphold the rules, regulations, and constitution of your appointing entity to secure its safety, and prosperity and thereby ensure its perpetuity as a thriving enterprise.

8. **Execution**: The processes involved in carrying out the implementation of your appointing entity's plans, ideas, and strategies that are committed to your leadership in answer to an exemplification of its reasons for deciding on you as one of its leaders.

9. **Management**: The acts and operations newly appointed leaders engage in to supervise accomplishment of various administrative details under their purview; performing them efficiently and effectively according to the appointing authority's expectations.

10. **Administration**: The secretarial, correspondence, and clerical (and clergy) details required to effect smooth operation and direction of new leaders' appointing entity's resources and forces delegated to leadership appointees to oversee and utilize.

11. **Ministry**: Professional functions that officially appointed leaders to rely on to uphold and circulate as their appointing entity's brand. Extends to modeling its style, materials, publications, organs, advertisements, responsibly. Everything that is concentric to protecting its public image and guarding its reputation throughout its communities.

12. **Servanthood**: The mentality new leaders should embrace for conscientious and subordinate attitudes that adopt and maintains a servant/service approach to the activities carried out for others as duly appointed leaders. Involves in prioritizing appointing entity's relief, comfort, business success. Comprises as well as doing or initiating what establishes or firms up its status as a credible provider in its field.

13. **Aptitude**: The multifaceted compound of gifts, talents, skills, and abilities that qualify you as a leader able to fill the voids and purposes your appointing entity selected you to cover and prosper on its behalf. Achievable by discovering and performing the feature, aspects, functions, and entrustments that define and justify your position.

14. **Attitude**: The mentality, emotions, and perspectives you demonstrated that qualified you for your promotion to remedy and repair the areas and issues your appointer's authorized you to handle on its behalf, with the expectation that they will

flourish under you as one of their leaders. Dependent upon your conformance to leadership's core requisites, which are its stature, reliability, and integrity, all affirmed by your consistency, continuity, and dignity in action. Effectively, these are evaluable as follows: your executivity, sense of responsibility, in-service conduct and behavior, professional mannerisms and protocols, the guidance of those up lead, accountability to your organization and any other characteristic integral a leadership position. Respond to the following based on what you read so far. Treat this assignment as a workshop and process your reading through each one of the 5HK's below.

➲ How to *think* it: Passing on what you learn to others.

➲ How to *act* on it: Engaging intelligences gained in practical situations:

➲ How to *share* it: Imparting the advantages and benefits gained from reading in social and communal environments.

➲ How to *build* on it: Expanding and edifying others with what you learned.

➲ How to *sustain* what is built: Methods & maneuvers that launch repair and restoration.

Thinking It Through, Working It Out, Assimilating It

Remembering that this is an inbuilding and upbuilding program designed to do more than inform you as a new leader, take a reading break and handle the following.

I will process this information by:

a) _____
b) _____.
c) _____.

Process I will adopt the following to my leadership role:

Step I. _____
Step II. _____.
Step III. _____.

Ways I will put forth the following efforts to increase my adaptability to this wisdom.

Step I. _____.
Step II. _____
Step III. _____.

CHAPTER 5

WHAT IT MEANS TO BECOME A LEADER

Leadership places enormous and stunning demands upon people in general. You quickly find out how what you thought it would mean to be out front and highly visible is only a fraction of the story. Your prior notions of leadership may have seen its work from a primarily public appearance perspective. The reality of your promotion no doubt altered that view extensively.

Leaders elevated to and office must accept that promotion *will* shift their lives and they must accept that is what it is supposed to do. New leaders should expect and plan for far-reaching life shifts after promotion primarily because it makes them an official leader in the kingdom. As they acclimate to their new post, newcomers to the leader will  find that time and attention will become scarce and that everything they do must be done efficiently and responsibly. You will read more on this later. Regardless of what a leader is being installed to do, the measure of authority delegated is fast recognized by all of the leader's associates, affiliates, and subsidiaries

Promotion Creates a New Life Form in a World

Persons being elevated to leadership experience something akin to a new life being born into the world. Normal duties and functions are expanded and diversified, taking on characteristics and demands tantamount to a whole new life. Progression is why roles such as the one you are taking on are designated a "lifestyle occupation." It is also why promotion to an office one a public servant. In the church or high government, the leader can become a minister. In secularity, one can be classified as a civil servant. Either way, the new leader's service obligations will put great stress the old life's norms. But consider this, not all stress is bad; some of it is vital to the growth and strengthen newcomers' overall leadership capabilities. They define and support latent capacities aroused by the promotion. Their appearance gives the new leader opportunity to solidify what works in an elevated position that was probably hardly noticed before promotion. Awakening talents and realizations permit enhanced discernment and focus attention on what is to be, shifting it away from what once was. New leaders should think about the natural abilities and acquired skills they bring to their position to draw on their potential. Once they do, the process of cultivating what their promotion relies on is next. For new leaders to succeed and bear lasting fruit to the Lord, they need to add solid qualities to their aesthetic behaviors as well. Here is a list of cultivatable potential new leaders should identify and sharpen as they grow in their new roles:

1. **Mental Powers** – the energy to think differently and will to focus on tasks at hand. Exemplify:
   _____.

2. **Memory Perception** – the acuity to discern and detect rightly judge and relate, restrain reactions until all available details are gathered and evaluated.

Illustrate: _____.

3. **Reason** -- Intellectual and emotional senses that probe, analyze, deduce and otherwise figure things out before accepting them as normal and making them the premise or impulse for issues and their solutions.

Describe: _____.

4. **Speech Skill** – Articulation is the key to this ability. Calls for being able to communicate intelligently, clearly devoid of superfluous harangues.

Exemplify: _____.

5. **Wealth Generation** – Acceptance that success and money go hand in hand, where the latter confirms the former: money symbolizes success in some way.

Approach: _____.

6. **Expertise** – Knowledge capacitated by knowhow that exhibits proficiency in an area or function. Goes to the aptitude, aptness, dexterity, and fitness of the leader in action.

Depict: _____.

7. **Capability** – Qualifiable potentiality that arises from experience and facility.

Portray: _____.

8. **Powers of Mind** – Mental fortitude, resilience, ration, and the like available and responsive to the leader when called upon.

Exhibit: _____.

9. **Habits of Mind** – The customary way the mind accepts and acts on information arising from its typical train of thought, instinctual reflexes and motivations, and fundamental pursuits and expectations from life.

Rationalize: _____.

10. **Functional Performance Ability** – Practical, efficient, operational agility that reliably direct and undergirds new leader efforts and pursuits.

Stage: _____.

Do Your Home Work Before Promotion

To manage the inevitable stress of change that comes with elevation, new leaders' lives, must set their lives and homes in order. They should speak honestly with their family members, letting them know that this is not a trial but a triumph for them. They need to communicate what it will take and how it will affect, although also reward, the household when they are promoted to leadership. It is important for Christian leaders to walk their families through how their obedience and service will put them squarely in the will of God. Partner with family members on the necessary adjustments that will enable the entire family to answer its calling and fulfill the will of God for it. Be mature about their responses and remember people react to change drastically sometimes. For instance, teens and youngsters will see it as the end of their world and an intrusion into their perfectly manageable life. Spouses may envision marital neglect and fear being demoted to second place in the leader's life behind the ministry. Extended family may feel threatened as cherished traditions and events seem to be at risk because of the leader's new demands. Friends are likely to feel that the leader is dropping them and leaving them without the companionship and social or recreational activities that define their friendship. The list can go on, but the message is clear. We revisit this subject later in the tutorial to expand your insight and equipment in this area.

Consider the Situation This Way

People dislike change and they show that dislike in a myriad of ways ranging from rage and tantrums to pouting and withdrawal. Some of them become moody and reclusive, declining to voice what they feel because of anger, a sense of futility, or simply because they cannot put what's going on inside them into words. As a result, new leaders should expect a span of emotions to wade through to get their family members accustomed to their new lives. One thing the new leader should not do is give in to their beloved ones antics and disobey the Lord. That would be detrimental to the new leader and the family. Instead, the promoted leader should see family and friend reactions as the first of many, many, emotional development skills needed to draw on as a leader. After all, new leaders will likely counsel others on these same issues. Some may be expected to help distressed parents deal with their turbulent teens. Others may assist with frustrated spouses, or vehemently opposing friends. Depending upon the position, some new leaders can be asked to mediate marital conflicts or pray couples through hard times. It could be you that helps with families in crises or guide others into decisions that will without a doubt disrupt their households. Your initiation to the world of leadership is good training for all of these future requirements. Seeing that such functions may be in the new leaders' future, now would be a good time to get comfortable and proficient at them.

First Responses to Your Rise

Startling you will find very mixed responses to your rise. Some of your coworkers and colleague will congratulate you. Others may deride you, being threatened and offended by your promotion. You should know that both are normal and should be respected and you cannot use either response to the measure of your readiness or leadership right to the ranks of leadership. Your views will change as you respond to your appointment. For instance, the people you formerly admired or criticized look quite impressive in their leadership roles. Their apparent handling of the job appears more skillful than you when first judged it to be because being on the other side you clearly see what it takes for them to carry out their duty day in and day out. A real, world vision of what it's like in leadership quickly takes hold to lessen your previous judgments and convictions on other's service.

You are now the one that gets to recover from the estrangement of those who once loved and appreciated you. You are now the friend or coworker turned leader that they are withdrawing from one by one. Those who know you well now criticize <u>you</u> for taking seriously, what you were promoted to do, either by avoiding you or shortening their encounters with you. Why? Because they now fear the inherent authority of your position, imagining it can and may do them harm in the future. To be honest, their concerns are not entirely baseless. Your loyalty to them must of necessity, give way to allegiance to the organization entrusting you with their leadership. It does not matter that you are unsure of what your appointment to leadership means, or your uncertainty over why they chose you. The fact is they did choose you and those you leave behind to become their leader will harbor no such confusion. Countless, unspoken changes will take hold in them due to the following ways their perceptions and opinions of you are altered.

First.	
Second.	
Third.	

Ministry's New Day

A new ministry age is upon us. Years of prophecy foretelling God's new day for His church and the world are come to pass. Indeed, the former things are to be no more. We are constantly reminded that the church's old, casual way of doing things is over and its lenient attitudes about everything God, rapidly becoming passé. The departures of major ministerial strongholds and the fall or falling away of once highly prestigious ministries signify how church or kingdom is done is drastically changing. And, with what is emerging as the contemporary church, it should. With the old guard rapidly vacating their spots, no duty is more pressing upon today's leaders than putting the right people in the right place at the right time. The right people, in the right place, at the right time. Extensive discussion n the three "rights" comes at the end of this guide. Compounding the problem is the notorious discredit brought on by irresponsible and immoral leaders. The incompetencies of the fruit they bear leaves a bad taste in the mouths of many, still passionately in love with the Lord and His church.

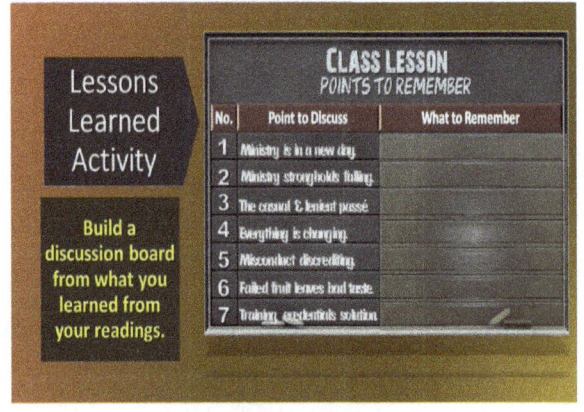

How We Got Here & God's Response

When God's people shun His wisdom and knowledge, He permits them to come under poorly trained or underage leaders. The Prophet Isaiah says this is a consequence of abandoning Him and His ways. That is where we are today. The popular trend of appointing the inexperienced to occupy serious ministry posts indifferent about proven track records or credentials that ascertain and confirm capabilities is disturbing. So widespread is the practice that leaders and appointers of this ilk have effectively destabilized the Lord's church. In doing so, they have, ruined many His people and jeopardize Christian security in this and the afterlife. To prevent or reverse the declining character of the church, caused by shortsighted and irresponsible practices, extreme overhauls that revamp presently entrenched methods must happen. It is no longer acceptable to authorize leadership entrants with weighty responsibly without reliable mechanisms in place to avert their downfall or perversion of Christ's ministries and spoiling His church. Such 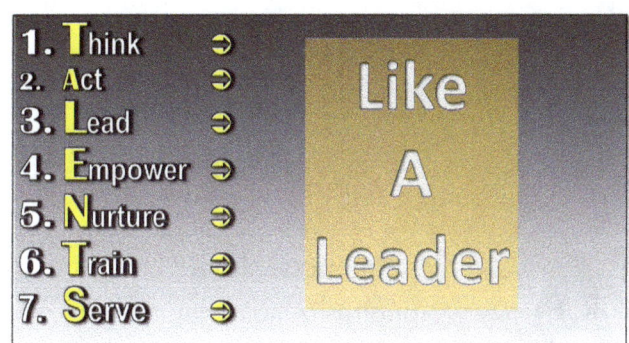 mechanisms should consist of set criteria, measurability gauges, checks and balances, inspections and inspectors, correctors and verifiers, and various forms of disciplinary and remedial protocols to maintain standards and uniformity. These instruments may be thought of as "the currencies of quality leadership."

In the contemporary church that is not always, or typically the case. The spearhead of such systems begins with educating, proving, and grooming those to take the reins of the Lord's church beforehand. Delegating power by appointing leaders prematurely devastates their followers and eventually the premature leader too. Prudence dictates that appointers verify their candidates' eligibility. Incompetence, lack of knowledge, and inexperience should be identified and corrected before handing over the reins of power or the lives of those to be led. If now, in the long run, the unproved will discredit their appointers causing others to suspect their right to choose leaders for them.

CHAPTER 6
LEADERSHIP APPOINTER WISDOM

As a rule, appointers should know and have gained twice as much experience as those they appoint. Also, they should forego installing or acquiescing to novices' insistence on sidestepping processes that set them in position equipped and qualified. It is foolhardy not to do so because when the unprepared falter, those they were to lead question why their incoming leader was ever appointed over them. Should this become a practice, followers will begin to distrust the judgment of appointers that constantly put the untried in power to their disadvantage. All of these factors are forcing change on us whether we want or are ready for it. Mistrust bred by the unaccountable and resentment over hasty appointments and ordinations reveals serious flaws in old church traditions, particularly independent churches. To these add, for the right reasons. Yet there is one more ingredient, putting today's and tomorrow's leaders, in and out of the church, in their right places the right way. All of these speak to ministerial licensing and ordination, and the practices used to accomplish them.

God's Leadership Proving, Pruning, Appointment Methods

Scripture records and narrates God's methods of leadership appointment to us a guide to how He does it. His Scriptures show how He elevates and appoints people to His leadership strata. He does so by first putting the candidate through rigorous trials. Once they are passed, then comes promotion. Proverbs says in 15:33 and 18:12 "before honor comes humility". That is to say, instruction and wisdom must precede promotion to remove destructive and counterproductive attitudes born of haughtiness. These must be dissolved before appointing leaders to their posts. The Apostle Peter adds to the mix, the fiery trials which are to test God's people. He phrases it as if these trials are commonplace and to be anticipated by those seeking promotion in God. Jesus discloses that His future leaders must successfully come through Satan's wheat-like sifting to confirm their eligibility and power to overcome and overrule him. These are but a few of God's way of pruning and readying a leader for His service.

Not long after learning of God's call on their lives, the Almighty's future leaders undergo the strenuous pruning to turn them into the faithful courageous leaders His people need, and that He can rely on ministerially. The Lord's model surfaces with Abraham and his sons, Joseph, Moses, David, and Samuel, the Lord Jesus His Son and His twelve apostles and beyond. Those familiar with God see the wisdom of His policy and practices. They know how dangerous novices can be and how weak and unstable underdeveloped leaders perform. As a case in point, compare the Lord's lengthy preparation of David in contrast to Saul's speedy coronation and ascent to Israel's throne.

Evidently, God planned David's ascent to Israel's throne was to an experienced and competent one. Naivete or incapably on David's part would not do for the man after God's own heart. So God put Israel's second king through nearly two decades of grueling hardship to assure his success as a ruler. Saul's success in comparison appears not to be as important. The first king to sit on the throne in God's stead was handpicked, anointed, installed, and left on his own to rule the nation, virtually overnight. It could be said that God made Saul king to disappoint His people enough to crave His righteous ruler waiting in the wings, so to speak. His nation's first king's poor leadership vindicated His preferred leadership style and guaranteed His people would appreciate the good king He really had in store for them. The Lord's methods have not changed over the ages, and they remain the same today.

Suspend your reading for a moment and complete the following "Probative[6] Exercise." Use what you just gained from the reading so far to conceive God's how's and why's of His leadership choices. Follow the selection guide below. Check the boxes that best serve your purposes. However, you must choose at least four. Upon choosing those you desire,

---

[6] Probative, belonging to proof; prove. Tending to prove a particular proposition or to persuade of truth. Exploration that substantiates. Tried, tested; evaluated, demonstrated. Put to the test in order to show and thereby convince.

proceed to create a leadership selection profile based on what you just read. Devise your profile as a leader would, styling it for use to assess your prospective leadership candidates. Select those that spoke to you most during the reading.

> ☐ Explore ☐ Enactment ☐ Inclination ☐ Retaining Knowledge ☐ Cases Study and Assessment ☐ Critical Thinking ☐ HK Drills ☐ Unit Content Scenarios ☐ Inspired Handling Necessary Change ☐ Dealing with Typical Leadership Simulations ☐ Experimenting with New Ideas ☐ Applying Scripture ☐ Relating Reading to Your Position ☐ Identifying and Recognizing Appropriate Assessment Tools and Utilities. ☐ Gauging and Measuring Success ☐ Recognizing Quality ☐ Recognizing Deficiencies and Correcting Them ☐ Spotting Promising Talent and Cultivating It ☐ Getting the Floundering and Wayward Back on Track ☐ Transferring Goals and Objectives to Action ☐ Assessing Outcomes ☐ Discovering Setups, Setbacks, Shortfalls ☐ Identifying and Solving Conflicts

If you are a class or training group, compare notes, share thoughts, explain or justify selections and clarify what motivated you to take the direction, path or course of action you chose. After completing this exercise, resume your reading.

PLOTTING YOUR LEADERSHIP PATH FROM YOUR READINGS

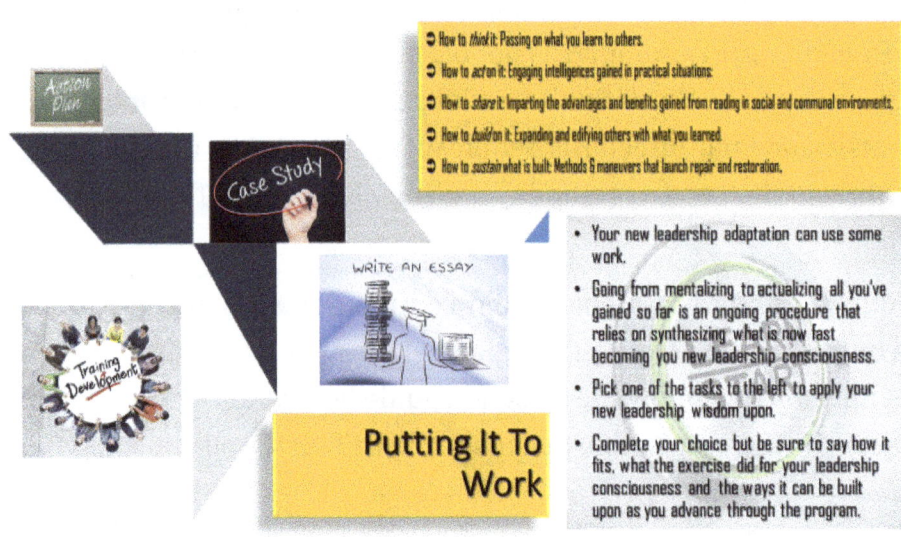

CHAPTER 7

YOUR THINKERS

Actionable Thoughts the Reading Imaged and Triggered in You So Far

This collection of thought provocative activities is intended to solidly embed the points and principles of the reading in your understanding. The idea is to accelerate your "responsive thinking" to do more with the material than review it for later recall. With assimilation that adapts you to the world of leadership as this guide's main objective, outlining and assigning after-reading actions and initiatives is a major step toward this end. Guided by it, turn your attention to the mental images and, what your reading triggered in your mind as a result. As you move through the section, pay attention to moments of reflections when you paused to think on some particular statement that struck your new leader chord. Enlightened by new thoughts and ideas that emerged from what you just took in, address each of the T.R.A.C.K. acronyms (spelled out by the bold letters). Draw on all you have gained so far in the tutorial.

How to *think* it: Passing on what you learn to others.

Mental Images & Answers Triggered in:

Thoughts ☐ **R**ationale ☐ **A**nswers ☐ **C**omprehensions ☐ **K**nowledges ☐ **E**quipment ☐ **R**ealizations ☐ **S**olvables ☐

As I read through this section, the thought that *imaged* in my mind was:

TRAINING SUPPLEMENT   NOW THAT YOU ARE A LEADER   PRICE UNIVERSITY

First.	
Second.	
Third.	

Rationale Reading Nurtured

This reading increased my appreciation of leadership rationale in the following ways:

Questions Reading Answered

First.	
Second.	
Third.	

Comprehensions Gained from Reading

Fourth.	
Fifth.	
Sixth.	

Knowledges Gained from Reading

Fourth.	
Fifth.	
Sixth.	

Equipment Gained from Reading

First.	
Second.	
Third.	

Solvables Derived from Reading

Created 2014 ©, Revised 2019 ©
Dr. Paula A. Price, PhD
All Rights Reserved

First.	
Second.	
Third.	

THE ACTORS

Actions, Actionizers, and Actionables Inspired By Your Reading

Everything about leadership is action. From the moment of promotion or appointment up to your first day's engagement in its affairs. Everything has to do with action, and that means actors. Those people that make up the collective hearts, heads, hands, and feet mobilized by your new authoritative voice. For that is what gradually happens when you enter the world of leadership. Your voice gets anointed by the sound of its sphere of the domain. The inner leader in you takes on a new tenor that resonates to others beneath their awareness, and yet taps their acknowledgment. The new sound that accompanies a leadership appointment penetrates that part of people that is programmed for the obedience that gets things done; that achieves and accomplishes. This group hears and heeds authority when it speaks, which is why and how you became a leader in the first place. Your readiness to be appointed pierced the followers sound and resounded in your appointers' ears as one possessing the potential to move others to action.

Leadership, you should also know as you undertake this task, is more than bossiness. Its sound is weighty, impelling, and convincing, but its intonation, though impelling, is motivational. In this regard, leaders speak to actionize, and the best ones do so by inciting more cooperation than intimidation. Concisely, what it means to have a voice of authority. And, you should also know that a commanding voice and an authoritative voice are not expressly the same. Commands compel for all sorts of reasons, fear, threat, bullying, etc. On the other hand, *authority*, which is always derived, adds a dimension of representational legitimacy, logic, license. Representational in this context meaning in the stead of another to whom the leader owes allegiance and obligation. These, I call this acronym Leadership's R.O.B.E.'s of delegation: Responsibility, Obligations, Benefits, Elegance.

Responsibility = Duties; Obligations = Conscientiousness; Benefits = Advantages; Elegance = Smartness

While leadership tonality is intrinsically commanding, its syntax [7] is wisdom. Leaders have acute wisdom that pierces normal, trendy, or cultural human rationale, going to the heart and soul of perplexing issues others skate over in their answers. The articular distinction is one that followed the appointed leader most of the life, subtly being sought out and heeded without explicit cause. People inexplicably the leader's voice in you and complied with its judgments, counsel, and correction. Sensing the difference more than realizing it, those seeking a credible leader discerned your capacity for getting others to surrender their will to your wisdom.

In this set of actionizers, use what you read so far as theory, so to speak to translate into actions that facilitate new leaders' adaption to leadership's unfamiliar roles. Completing this exercise helps you commence your leadership experience with more than subjective thoughts in mind and fantastical feelings in the heart. Handling action items like this one lays the groundwork for your future planning, strategizing, and decision-making obligations. They forge viable links between what you are responsible for as a leader and your methods of laying out the best ways to do it.

How to *act* on it: Reading discussions that enlarge intelligences:

○ Instill, ○ Install ○ Inseminate, ○ Instruct, ○ Institute, ○ Implement

What the Reading Instilled in Me:

As I read through this section, the information most instilled[8] in my leadership self is:

What the Reading Installed[9] in Me:

As I read through this section, the strengths and faculties reading installed in my leadership are:

---

[7] Rules of composing and arranging words.
[8] Imparted, implanted, inculcated, drilled, impressed (or pressed into me).
[9] Connected, fitted, fixed, embedded, established, positioned in me as a leader.

1.	
2.	
3.	

What Reading Most Inseminated in Me:

As I read through this section, what was most deeply inseminated my leadership makeup is:

Most Instructional Statements

As I read through this section, what I found most instructional is:

1.	
2.	
3.	

Appreciation of Leadership as a Broad Range Scopic Institution

As I read through this section, what took my perception of leadership from a personal endeavor or initiative to an institution one is:

Reading Implementation

As I read through this section, the statements that inspired my implementation ideas are:

1.	
2.	
3.	

THE TRANSMITTERS

Carriers, Communicators, Broadcasters, Publishers

How to *share* it: Steps to extending what you read and now understand to others.

TRAINING SUPPLEMENT　　　NOW THAT YOU ARE A LEADER　　　PRICE UNIVERSITY

○ Talk Out ○ Write Out ○ Publish ○ Broadcast ○ Advise ○ Coach ○ Educate ○ Correct ○ Train

As a "Talk It Out" approach my reading conversational points begin with:

1.	
2.	
3.	

As a "Write It Out" approach my reading summarization focus begin with:

1.	
2.	
3.	

As a "Publish It" approach my reading circulation plan begins with:

1.	
2.	
3.	

In taking a "Broadcast" approach my reading showcase elements will contain:

1.	
2.	
3.	

In taking an "Advisement Tool" approach my reading counseling points begin with:

1.	
2.	
3.	

In taking a "Coaching Tool" my reading mentor concentrations begin with:

1.	
2.	
3.	

In taking an "Educational" approach my reading lesson plans begin with:

TRAINING SUPPLEMENT   NOW THAT YOU ARE A LEADER   PRICE UNIVERSITY

1.	
2.	
3.	

As a "Corrector" approach my reading disciplines or developers begin with:

1.	
2.	
3.	

In taking a "Trainer's" approach my reading show points begin with:

1.	
2.	
3.	

UPBUILDING AND BROADENING

How to *build* on it: Expanding and edifying others with what you learned.

○ Reconsider ○ Sift ○ Identify ○ Review ○ Reevaluate ○ Assessors ○ Revisions ○ Determinations ○ Developments ○

What I read so far caused me to reconsider the following preconceptions or preconditioning:

1.	
2.	
3.	

While going through this material I found myself sifting through the following thoughts and sentiments:

1.	
2.	
3.	

As I read through this material, I was able to identify the following unrealized things about my leadership perspectives and beliefs:

1. _____
2. _____
3. _____

To confirm my understanding and reconcile previous readings on this subject I reviewed and compared the following:

1. _____
2. _____
3. _____

To take stock of where I was as a leader or newcomer to leadership, I reevaluated the following issues I brought to my promotion:

1. _____
2. _____
3. _____

I intend to use the following criteria and metrices to assess my present and preferential leadership style and values:

1. _____
2. _____
3. _____

My reading motivated me to make the following revisions in my leadership perceptions:

1. _____
2. _____
3. _____

To fortify my decisiveness as it will be needed in my approach to leadership, I am determined to adapt or adopt the following:

1. _____
2. _____
3. _____

In preparation to develop myself and those under my leadership, I will employ and engage in the following to succeed as a leader:

1. _____
2. _____
3. _____

CHAPTER 8

THE CONSTRUCTORS AND EXPANDERS

Upbuilding and Broadening

✪ How to *sustain* what is built: Methods and maneuvers that launch, repair and restore.

○ Galvanize ○ Guard ○ Recover ○ Drill ○ Repair ○ Embed ○ Acclimate ○ Sensitivity

In taking a "*Galvanizer*" I will electrify my reading dynamics with:

1.	
2.	
3.	

As a "*Guardian*" of this wisdom while applying to my leadership development and methodologies, I intent to:

1.	
2.	
3.	

To "*Recover*" what my promoters expect me to recoup as a leader, I will use my readings to equip my supervisees and my leadership environment with the following:

1.	
2.	
3.	

As a "*Drills*" tool to get to the root of my leadership and its effects on others, as well as its attainments, I will use my reading to:

1. _____
2. _____
3. _____

As a "*Repair*" approach my reading show points begin with:
1. _____
2. _____
3. _____

Spurred by my readings, I will "*Embed*" its teachings by driving home its principles and putting them to practice in the following ways:
1. _____
2. _____
3. _____

To "*Acclimate*" myself to leadership and my team to the style I cultivated from my readings, I will:
1. _____
2. _____
3. _____

To nurture the "*Sensitivity*" new leaders should possess and maintain, I will extract from my reading the following ideals:
1. _____
2. _____
3. _____

STUDY NOTES & REFLECTIONS

_____
_____
_____
_____
_____
_____

Now to resume your reading.

CHAPTER 9
WHO CAN AND SHOULD COUNT ON YOUR LEADERSHIP

The hardest part of becoming a leader is the sweeping ways your loyalties and affections must change. Even if you are unaware of it in the beginning, it won't be long before you realize you are changing, in spite of your best efforts not to do so. Those promoting you to leadership expect to see and be able to note your growth and transformation. On the other hand, many of those you leave behind resent it. For a good period of time, it will seem as if you can't please anybody, not even your family if you have one. Early joy and respect over your elevation often turn into anger and disapproval. Still, if you are going to remain in the post, you must navigate hostile waters and maneuver around disgruntled souls to prove to yourself and others you really are the one. Early in your transition period, you must demonstrate you are well able to win most of your leadership opinionators over. That is the only way to establish or restore peace in your world. What does it all require? A major factor in your leadership adjustment period is your family and home life. Regardless of how often we hear "family first", the truth is it is not possible or realistic. Here are some reasons why.

Family First, Really?
The notion of putting your family first above all else is a noble one, and nothing in this discussion suggests you should relegate them to nothing as you pursue and fulfill your career. But you should not delude yourself or mislead them into thinking that life, as it was, will always be. If you are a prudent person, you will walk them through what must

change, ask their help in keeping important things the same, and the most critical of it all, earn and retain their respect. In your candid discussions with your family, you have to somehow gain their confidence in your promotion, that it may change you for the better and not for their worse. Guide their reactions and opinions by frankly letting them know you can master your new world with them behind you and at your side. Solicit their advice to counteract their fears. Involve them in how you face your new challenge. Let them know you need their wise input to balance your love and attention to them with the duties that can make life better for them in the world. In communicating these things to them, use the following as your list of non-negotiables, placed upon you as a new leader. Draw on them for answers and action to the following. Your family must accept and orientate to the following by you, ideally in advance of your promotion.

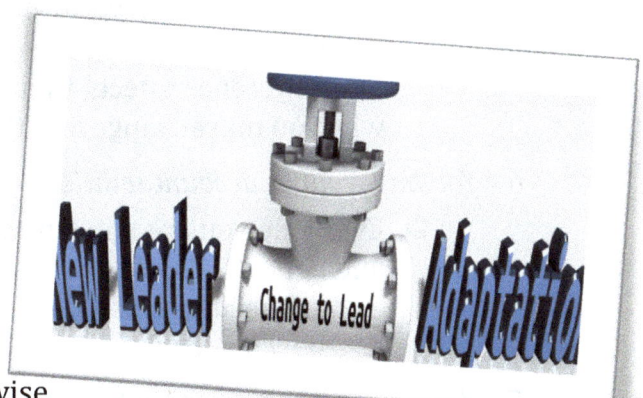

Twelve Ways You Must Prime Your Family for Your Leadership

1. *Your promotion brings with it weightier and higher demands.*
    - ⊃ What your promotion expects and requires of you.

2. *You have new work rules.*
    - ⊃ Specify old rules that changed when you were promoted. Justify the ones that directly, and may at times adversely, affect them.

3. *You have people under and over you relying on you.*
    - ⊃ The most influential new characters in your new work life and your interactions with them should be named and their function in your new leadership world stated and discussed.

4. *You have increased responsibilities.*
    - ⊃ Leadership obligations you cannot dismiss that may overlap onto your customary family regimens must be frankly identified. Family input should be encouraged, but not taken as alternatives to what you cannot alter.

5. *You are no longer merely a worker but are now a leader.*
    ⮞ The primary differences between when you were a worker or follower and you as a leader have to be extensively said and their actions portrayed. Family members should be aware of what will make you different and how that difference affects them and their world. They should be informed of why you must change and the role you need then to play in that change.

6. *You have higher accountabilities.*
    ⮞ Everyone you are now answerable to and who is answerable to you above and beneath should not be mysteries to your family. Instead, share as much as they need to grasp the scope and nature of answerability put upon you as a new leader.

7. *You have new timelines to honor.*
    ⮞ The ways your time, especially your free time must change, the reasons and the ways you are asking them to honor what you cannot dishonor as a new leader. Hash it out and be creative in your explanations and persuasions.

8. *You must be at work at thus and thus time.*
    ⮞ The rigid versus flexible work schedule you must maintain as a new leader.

9. *You must work for so many hours.*
    ⮞ The conditions under which you must put in additional work hours as a new leader and the solutions your family can help you work out to balance work demands against your time with them.

10. *You have such and such days off, and as a leader, they are not etched in stone.*
    ⮞ Your flexible and schedulable off days and your inflexible ones, and how you can put in time with your family without compromising your position or sacrificing their contentment.

11. *Your position requires you to be available for the reasons you were promoted.*
    ⮞ Clarify with your family the relevant obligations that come with your promotion. Talk it through with them, hear them out, and jointly come up with ways to reduce the disruptions in your family life. At the same time, press to gain their concessions if you cannot entirely win them over in order to keep the peace in your household.

12. *You may have take-home work those of your household ought not to criticize you for doing on their time.*
    ⮕ Explain the take-home work you may have from time to time. But it may be wise to avoid doing so as much as possible. If there is take work home you should bear the brunt of its disturbances. Try not to inflict its unpleasantness on your household.

With respect to these concerns and consequences to your leadership promotion, the answer to family time could be putting in more hours at work, staying up after family goes to bed, or leaving early in the morning to get it done. Any of these approaches could pacify the situation. What you want to do, however, is to resist the temptation to resent the promotion because of your family's reactions or resent your family because of your elevation in life. Bitter thoughts may come, relentless frustrations can nag you. But you have the upper hand. So if God ordained the promotion you can rest assured, He engrafted in you everything you will need to excel in it.

However, you should know and accept that leadership is burdensome. The weight of its inconveniences is largely borne by the appointed leader, which is why the sphere of leadership is described as weighty. You are the one to make it work for more than yourself and your own. To make it work, you do so by honoring your word and keeping up your responsibilities to your appointers. Remember they are entrusting you with a measure of their entity's stability and prosperity. That trust should not be disdained, and its responsibilities should not be shirked. The truth is innate leaders are a unique breed. Their handling of life shows their exceptionality. If you are reading this material and have gotten this far, you can pretty well accept that you are a credible leader from the inside out, or you have the potential to become one. These are but a few of the issues that await you when you step into the world of leadership. If you were chosen for it, then something in you says you can work it out. After all, winning over those who love and need you fortifies your abilities to win over those who do not.

Task: Develop a profile to assess yourself as a leader the first 90-days. Check the boxes that apply—at least four—and proceed to create a personal assessment out of those you choose. Lay it out as a leader would and style it in a way that you can use to assess your supervisees. Select those that spoke to you most during the reading.

Anticipate and Prepare

Layout below, how you intend to present and resolve these with your family.

PRESENTING MY NEW LEADERSHIP POSITION REQUIREMENTS TO MY FAMILY
1.
2.
3.
4.
5.
6.
7.
8.
9.
10.
11.
12.

Other Thoughts on the Matter of Family

Earlier sections introduced this discussion. You were given a little background, some insights, and pointers. Then you were told that the family subject would be revisited. Here is where we do so. To pick where we left off and to clarify or expound on an earlier point, you should know that new leaders shifting from their old station to the new one must do so with its impact on their family in mind. Born leaders are peculiarly built to take this in stride. No doubt, they have faced off with opposition to their destiny in the past. History with diverse reactions to their advancement in life eases the acclimation burdens that come with promotion. That is not to say they are immune to their family's displeasure. It is to say they are experientially equipped to work through it, ideally to everyone's benefit. The other type of leader is the trainable one. This leader may emerge late in life, take classes that *enskills*[10] them with leadership principles and practices that make sense to them. The difference between the two is intuition and instinct overtraining and technique. The former is enhanced by the latter, but the latter can be devoid of the former and only rely on training recall for guidance and solutions. Leaders may be trained but they must desire and believe in their leadership from the heart otherwise hot and bitter emotions will inspire them to quit. Of all the groups to be distressed or blessed by your promotion is your family. Their world is sure to be turned upside down when you enter the world of leadership. Ignoring this inevitability could destabilize your household and make you an enemy of the home. Avoiding it calls for preparation that helps them adapt to "*life as they know it being no more.*"

To this end, leaders must have done, or do, the work of preparing their family for their rise in stature and status. Preparations are essential and critical because if family members are unprepared for the demands your promotion puts upon them, they will intentionally or not sabotage you because they resent your elevation. In addition, you too will have a very hard time changing into who and what you must become to fulfill your position and execute your post well. Upon promotion, several things emerge that you should be aware of when you become a leader. The main one is sabotage; the sabotage sparked by resentment and regret. Meanings of the word *sabotage* range from disruption to damage; to interference that causes interruption; they extend to harm and incapacitation all the way to impairment.

Take a moment and think of these terms and how they collectively reflect some or most of your sentiments on your new position and your family's reactions to it. Write what you suspect and know about both below.

MY NEW LEADERSHIP POSITION
My Thoughts & Feelings
My Family's Sentiments & Reactions

---

[10] Installed or inset ability acquired by training; ability to produce solution in problematic domains, acquired or innate. Author.

The Saboteur Influence & Effects of Both

Having completed the above exercise, you should be somewhat alerted to the underlying attitudes and reactions to your leadership you and your family share, and perhaps imprudently exchange. Both of your views are rooted in two things, nostalgia, and selfishness. Nostalgia because that is what family members use the most to guilt or intimidate rising leaders into giving and allowing them to keep the reins of power over your life. Let's have some fun by scripting and depicting some of the tactics your knowledge of your family could devise. Use the list below to imagine some of their possible nostalgia tactics:

> ➢ Celebrating and soliciting past memories,

Sample Depiction:
Possible Script:
Change Agent Response:

> ➢ Dragging out old pictures and recordings to arouse your desire to return to the fold.

Sample Depiction:
Possible Script:
Change Agent Response:

> ➢ Tying aforetime recollections to everything you must forego or limit.

Sample Depiction:
Possible Script:

Change Agent Response:

- Playing old-time songs and old school games meant to bring back old feelings,

Sample Depiction:
Possible Script:
Change Agent Response:

- Hosting commemorative events that conflict with your new schedule,
    - and then chide you for not attending.

Sample Depiction:
Possible Script:
Change Agent Response:

- Inviting old friends or holding gatherings at old haunts.

Sample Depiction:
Possible Script:
Change Agent Response:

- Summoning help from the most authoritarian, critical, and persuaders of the family.
    - Usually, these are patriarchs and matriarchs.

Sample Depiction:
Possible Script:

Change Agent Response:

- ➢ Warring against your leadership if they disagree with it
    - o using memories, tradition, enticements and

Sample Depiction:
Possible Script:
Change Agent Response:

Family and Friends Love Driven Backlash

Lastly and yet most indelibly are criticism and accusation. Criticism takes the form of guilt. Loved ones have been known to charge new leaders with abandonment because of their time with loved ones becomes less than they are accustomed to enjoying. If there was a pattern of family unity and fellowship. Some have claimed the new leader demoted their standing to be consumed with the promotion. Often disgruntled family and friends usually follow these claims up with charges of neglect; saying the attention they once got now goes to the new world and its communities. They see themselves as second or lesser in your eyes. Beyond this, the family will rival your leadership and compete with it using all sorts of events and behaviors that go so far as to disinvite you from regular outings or gatherings. Or ceasing to invite you at all.

To punish you for moving up in the world without them, family and friends may pretend to ignore you for your own good, so they say. When in reality, they really mean, it serves you right for deserting them. They want to convey to you that you deserve to be left out of their circle and happenings for violating the "family always comes first" rule. After all, it is not their fault you chose progress and betterment over loyalty and devotion to them. So what do you do? You outlast their cagey tactics knowing that they endure but for a while in your life. Keep that thought in mind. Life's cycles change and its pendulums swing back and forth. These means give it enough time and the tides invariably change direction and when they do, those caught in one swell can and often do change their minds. Next, I discuss self-celebrating and self-deprecating leaders.

CHAPTER 10
THE SELF-CELEBRATORY AND SELF- DEPRECATING LEADERS

New leaders are often unaware of how preconditioned their thoughts and emotions are when they enter leadership. Unless they have had solid prudent training, their preconceptions of higher positions are dangerously skewed. Numerous entrants to these positions are incognizant of what they really believe about leadership, expect or desire from it. To many newcomers, leadership is their chance, their opportunity to unleash their inner beast. Finally, they get to *boss* people around, parade and swagger around the facility.

Misguided new leaders upon being promoted rejoice with at last they are the ones out of the office and out of touch for reasons unknown. And, they get to unburden themselves of what they deem to be frivolous tasks and demanding work. Now they can hand it off to those beneath them. A ready-made set of subservience is on hand to provide personal services, rewards, and demands were waiting for their day. It is their turn to be served by others. They are recognized and honored. The list can go on, but you get the point. Self-serving celebratory leadership is the bane of follower's existence and a sure detriment to the newcomer who thinks that is the way.

But, leadership is not primarily about entering your day. It is about vision fulfillment, support, and collaboration. The rewards are more perks and compensation than they are tokens of prestige. Self-celebratory leader's perception of what it means to lead others is self-centered. Much of what they do is to feed the ego and reap the harvest on visions that become payoff or payback realities.

The self-celebratory leader is very public but not frequently involved. Being out front defines their leadership style more than cooperating with their team. It satisfies their affirmation hunger. These leaders are not collaborators and can often appear to be dictators: "Do what I say, handle what I give you and don't expect me to do your work. After all, I have a public to please and accolades to receive." Such leaders are absent, tardy, disengaged and consumed with touring the leadership circuit and connecting with those they admire, on the pretext of scouting business and making deals. Contacts are usually superficial, more in the self-celebrating leader's mind than in reality. Business is repeatedly said to be in the process of negotiation, and closure is not their strong suit. Appearance and prestige, reward and renown are top priorities; taking precedence over duty and responsibility.

In this scenario, accountability is nearly nonexistent as the strutting leader seizes every opportunity to remind all they that are in charge of should not be expected to comply with the requests or requirement of those they lead. Lastly, these leaders' actions are mostly self-centered. After all, they are ever in self-celebration mode. Therefore myopia dominates their initiatives and ventures and makes intolerance the norm for them. This what they want and everyone beneath better figure it out, work it out and take the hits for it. Everything is about them, so decisions, initiatives, and actions emerge from them and land on the organization's team. When asked for clarity to do their jobs, workers and followers are chided for needing direction and instruction. They are ridiculed or derided for asking for explanations, resources, and the like from their self-celebrating leader. Requests are met with or followed by snide remarks. They are scolded and told to figure it out themselves and cease bothering the leader with the mundanity of daily affairs. Many times this is because the leader does not have the answers to the questions. Typically, the methods escape them. Their capabilities are mostly the commands.

The Self-Deprecating Leader

The self-deprecating leader is likely to be the ministerial or social service servant or public advocate. The call to tend to the suffering and disadvantaged means to this leader that humility and piety represent their leadership style. These can be the most misleading and their reticence misconstrued, being taken as humility. At times these conclusions are true but in far too many cases they are simply misdirected. Naturally shy people have taken the self-deprecating posture to legitimize their timidity. Introverted souls cloak their uncertainties or sense of unworthiness with aloofness. A reserved exterior conceals inability to or disinterest in coming close to outsiders even if they are leading others. Getting these people to warm up to the position is an entirely different thing altogether. At first, the true reasons for their detachment must be identified. Is it because they are shy? Are they struggling with inferiority or insincerity? Are they actually the type of self-willed leader who long ago set limits on their sociability and fraternization with their staffs? If so, then irrational rigidity drives their meekness. Perhaps it is not really compassion. The last one could signal the leader's mastery of nonverbal control tactics. This type learns early to say all the right and tender things. Under closer observation, you find they are conspicuously doing good deeds that hardly ever chart. When they are out of touch or restrained, generally it can be because they are withdrawing for emotional reasons in support of their pretense.

A carefully contrived persona is obliging to their will to retreat from others to nurse their innate craving for aloneness. In this case, self-deprecation is used as a ploy to allow them to give as little as possible to get as much as they want in return. In short, the deprecation part gives them their way without conflict or resentment. People are instead sold on their soft tones, tender overtures, and pious conduct. So appreciative of their projected temperament are they that they never suspect possible underlying willfulness that controls through perception and conversation and not deeds. Another likelihood is the self-deprecating leader hates attention to the point of spurning it entirely. They renounce acknowledgment, detest being made a spectacle of accolades, and resist all attempts to publicly celebrate their achievements. In this regard such leaders can appear rude and abrasive, rebuking others admiration and condemning them for arousing or tempting their vigorously subdued pride. And not let us forget that in countless instances, humility, meekness, and piety are genuine attributes and demeanors that should be confused but not dismissed on suspicion only.

Another version of this demeanor is the leader that uses self-deprecation to hide utter contempt for others perceived as beneath them. These leaders are actually self-celebrating under the guise of self-deprecation. They snub others regard and respect, perhaps due to repeated injury over earlier pretentious experiences. Or, maybe they see themselves as unobligated to the rewards of their efforts. Either way, you would be wise to explore your submerged beliefs for the attitudes they incite and the behaviors they breed. You should be the one to discover or uncover your detriments and potential impediments. Not by those suffering and enduring them until they can no longer indulge your harsh and harmful idiosyncrasies. Just these descriptions alone can contribute to your new leaders' difficulties and adversity.

My Planned Talking Points:

- How to *think* it: Passing on what you learn to others.
- How to *act* on it: Engaging intelligences gained in practical situations:
- How to *share* it: Imparting the advantages and benefits gained from reading in social and communal environments.
- How to *build* on it: Expanding and edifying others with what you learned.
- How to *sustain* what is built: Methods & maneuvers that launch repair and restoration.

My Detectable Thought Processors:

First.	
Second.	
Third.	
Fourth.	
Fifth.	

My Discernible Emotional Sensors:

First.	
Second.	
Third.	
Fourth.	

CHAPTER 11
INITIAL ADVERSITY OFTEN HAS A SHORT SHELF LIFE

More than a few of those harboring hostility and disappointment at your decision will go back to their lives and business shortly after the tactics begin. They will get tired or find themselves no longer interested or able to attend the conspiracy meetings that plot their vengeance against your rise in life. Others will move away, and you will have surrendered to them for nothing. Still, more will get ill, pass away, or become motivated by your courage and pursue higher positions in life themselves. All it takes for you to ride out the storm is to determine to outlive their onslaughts. You can do this realizing that life and circumstances change quickly. Today, you are the target. Tomorrow, it will be someone else in the family tree or in the friendship circle.

Laying the Ax to the Root

Depending on the nature and scope of your family ties and values, their origins and covenants, any one of these actions can seed rejection in you and not long after that urge renouncement of your promotion. If you are not careful. Constantly feeding on loved ones' callousness and crucifying of your soul intends to bring you back into their fold: A lot humbler and grateful they received you back. Although you go along with it, your psyche will never be the same and soon you will blame them for the lost opportunity and its many rewards. Some you enjoyed as an achiever and others as potential prospects of your future. So, you will resettle into where you were before your promotion and loved ones will temporarily celebrate you doing so. But that won't last long because eventually, they will disrespect your decision to forsake your future and your success for them. Here is how it can surface.

At family gatherings when the subject of work and opportunities come up, they will insinuate how foolish they think you are for letting your promotion to a higher position go. Some will go so far as to say they would not have done it. As time passes, you hear negative and mocking or scolding comments that let you know they appreciate your return to them but disdain, your renouncement of your promotion for them. Mockery and scolding gradually give way to ridicule when you try to share or use some of the knowledge and experience you gained from your brief stint as a leader. Reactions to your attempts are met with indifference fueled by contempt over your succumbing to their taunts and harassment. You are scorned for not being able to stick with it and thereby earn the right to tell them anything. It just gets ugly from there. And then there is your side of the situation.

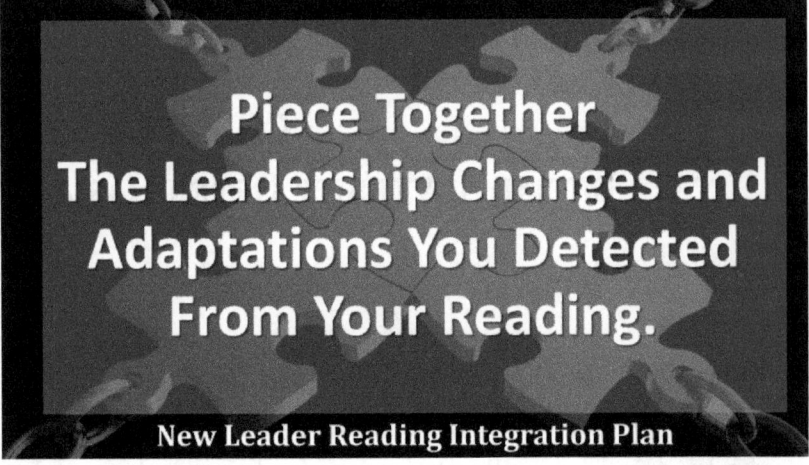

New Leader Reading Integration Plan

Sample Depiction:
Possible Script:
Change Agent Response:

What If You Become the Saboteur of Your Promotion?

Taking the same scenarios and turning them inward makes you the saboteur. You may become the one yearning to reverse the clock, inwardly wishing to turn it back to when you participated family customs and enjoyed freely engaging in them. How does this show up? Its number one and most impelling feeling is regret that changes into resentment. You dislike the hours, the added workloads, the endless meetings, and in your mind, the mind-numbing training that drags on and on. All you do in your new role is "do, do, do." Everywhere you turn, there is something for you **to do** that stills your time and chips away at former family relations. You begrudge missing family outings and gatherings despite your family understanding that you must. You fume inside over the changes that leadership imposes on you, feeling them unjust and not worth your time and energy. You let your unhappiness eke out. Your seething exposes itself in veiled ways. For instance, you complain in subtle ways only your team and those who promoted you discern. You say to yourself you have a life. You are not giving up everything for this promotion. You have a family and friends you want to spend time with; that you have no intention of forsaking for this job. Before your promotion, you had hobbies, ventures, adventures, and other interests that shouldn't be sacrificed or surrendered just because you became a leader. You love your downtime and dream of it constantly. You miss your end of workday routines: television, telephone, hanging out with so and so. Yes, at first you did appreciate the chance to move up in the company and the world, but at what cost.

What I read so far from this section, caused me to *reconsider* the following preconceptions or preconditioning:

First.	
Second.	
Third.	

The thought of cost hits at the crux of the matter: You failed to count the cost and now desperately wish you had because of what it will say about you if you quit and go back. Do you notice it is all about you and yours? Startlingly, everything boils down to just you alone. Your regret, your discontentment, your resentment and that of your family and friends. A once exciting memorable event in your life crumbles into dismay. Suddenly, you despise your elevation because those close to you did. You despise your promoters for putting you in such a position, making you a target of unpopularity. Your gratitude, once happily high, wanes under unanticipated duress. It seems all that surrounds you is misery and longing. Relentless inward struggles send you on a downward spiral; longing for your family consumes your thoughts and emotions. You have yet to acknowledge the great job they did of making your promotion all about them and their disapproval. Initial love and appreciation for the position you now hold are soured by the opposition you neither expected nor were equipped to tackle. The tension between the two, personal life and professional life, takes its toll on you.

For many new leaders, it tragically does. Believe this one thing though. At first former coworkers and colleagues will say they understand, at least to your face. But, out of your earshot, they joke about how you weren't able to make it because you never should have been promoted in the first place. Most of them will probably never admit they feel that way to your face, but rest assured a good number of them share the sentiment. Their compassion for your inability to stay in the position in some ways is just a veneer to cover how their hearts really judge your predicament. The illustrations you just read are meant to motivate you to guard against your own selfishness. Indulging it can fracture your certainty and confirm nostalgic selfishness introduced earlier is working you over.

Task: Sketch a short commentary on what you just read that opens with what you appreciate or fail to appreciate about it. End with what you envision doing with its wisdom.

A Point of Clarification

None of these illustrations are to suggest you should not want downtime, periods of rest and relaxation. Desiring both is normal and should happen at regular intervals. It is when they are nearly all you think about and plans for that it becomes a problem. Examples of obstructive focus on escapism are: You spend your free time, often your work time, planning vacations that are months. These habits take the place of supporting your team, upgrading your group, and managing your leadership responsibilities. You watch the clock for quitting time; and not so much for due dates and deadlines. You waste time mingling with your staff that in turn must lose productivity catering to your need for distraction. A tactic you use to offload the weight of the leadership position you now hold.

You skirt meetings and disparage your peers for their dedication. Seething inside, almost incessantly, you bemoan the loss of your old life and its entertainments. Or, you grumble about leaving your old world of isolation. Where you controlled everything. You did what you wanted when you felt like it, engaging in life or not on your own terms. Isolation in this respect refers to persistent seclusion from others. For some new leaders entering leadership's sphere from excessive aloneness where the less human contact they have the better, this spells trouble. Performance may be quality, but morale is usually low due to the leader's detachment from the team. These leaders fight unifying processes and balk at interruptions. They continually go on about how incompatible they are with leadership's invasion of their family recreations. They pileup hideaways they call getaways; retreats from reality and socialization that reach all the way back to childhood and adolescence. Generally, as incoming leaders, they bring to the position a lifetime of withdrawing from their world. From youth, it served as avoidance to dodge socializing with others. A habit that will irk and offend their followers who read their aloofness or hurried departure from gatherings as superiority or rejection.

Sometimes, the issue is just unmitigated shyness that was never dispelled. In many cases, the three, superiority, rejection and shyness take their turns motivating the distance some leaders put between themselves and their world. Judging from common excuses and explanations given for their conspicuous absences from other than compulsory events, concern for acquiring the post overrides developing subordinates while occupying it.

> Take a moment now to develop an assessment or interview tool that would extract information that discloses at least half of the preceding indicators at work in a new leader you just inherited from your oversight organization. Discuss your tool with class or peers if possible.

Other instances of being incompatible with a leadership promotion signifying lack of desire to conform to are consist of wanting to be off duty more than on. The prestigious part that persuaded you to take the position now appears to be not so prestigious at all. Being restricted to an office or other worksite loses its appeal. Being your own boss or being free to lead yourself and your life where and as you will begin to look very tempting to you. When you are off-duty, you forbid anyone to talk about work because you want to forget it for as long as you can. Ardently, you resist the very notion of anything pertaining to your promotion ever infringing on your "me time". Evasive maneuvers guard and protect former recreations you once enjoyed at will. While it may go on for a while, it cannot remain that way forever. Usually, it all comes to a head when you either, due to indulgent mental habits and excursions, cause a major crisis that reverberates on others and other areas of your sphere or department. Or, your when frequent absences or unpleasantries accompany being denied your way. Conduct such as this adversely affects morale and demotivates others who see your negativity justification for downgrading themselves. Increasingly, your mindset causes your attitude to deteriorate. Your performance and regard for your leadership suffer until you leave your appointers no recourse but to demote you. In view of these disclosures, be smart about promotion. Refuse to allow present momentary discomforts define your service or short circuit your ability to stay in the position. These could permanently block you from leadership ranks in the future.

CHAPTER 12
IT'S IN YOU TO PULL IT OUT; DON'T THROW IT AWAY

By now, it should be clear to you that successful leadership transition and conscientiousness ride on faithfulness, steadfastness, inner resolve, perseverance, and persistence, and nothing less. You know you already have these working within you. Or, how else did you qualify for your promotion? The bigger question then, or perhaps task, is how to dig these essentials from beneath the rubble of human sentiments bombarding you to benefit you, your organization, and those you lead. The answer is distance. Yes, it sounds ridiculous. But in the beginning, you need to put some distance between yourself and the relentless criticism, accusations, and constant resentment. Notice I said distance, not desertion. The distance should not cut you off from your people, merely give you space to think and process your prior and next steps.

> ### Take Distance Breaks
>
> In the beginning of your leadership, you need to put some distance between yourself and the relentless criticism, accusations, and constant resentment.

Taking such breaks from heated moments is useful. It helps you recuperate from the new leader barrages and keep a level head. Together, they improve the odds of making rational decisions, especially under pressure. For your sake and for the sake of those close to you, as much as possible, even if only inwardly at first, you need to maintain a healthy space between the negatives you can avoid from those bent on heaping them on you. Strategically scheduled separation from difficulties can calm your emotions and allow you to rediscover what qualified you to lead in the first place. Inner distancing may be all you can afford in the beginning. Physical distance may have to come later. Inner distancing means refusing to respond and react anything except what is beyond your control, or necessary to fulfill your position. It calls for choosing companions and comforters wisely to ensure you are surrounded by more encouragers than critics. Eventually, this tactic may cease to be necessary as you grow stronger and more confident. Until then though, during your separated times, seriously reflect on what is happening to, and in you. Process it for strength and power, not to regret your promotion or imagine quitting. You also do not want to unintentionally take it out on others because of anger and frustration. When you can get away physically do not do so with the folks you just left to become a leader. They may read your presence or invitation as secret disregard for your position and their duty to it.

Lastly is, whether figurative or actual this survival tactic should include turning in to the Lord from whom all promotions come. In addition, try very hard not to overwhelm your family with your new leader adjustments. They may not give you the encouragement and consolation you expect. And, you can't leave them behind; they live with you. Also, when things settle down, the family may hold a long-lasting grudge against your position, even if you get over its initial upsets. These are just a few new leader pointers, but you will discover more as you go along. Take a short break from your reading to respond to the following. Afterward, return to the reading.

As a *"Guardian"* of this wisdom, while applying to my leadership development and methodologies, I will draw on it to:

First.	
Second.	
Third.	

In taking a *"Mobilizer"* I will stimulate my reading discussers with:

First.	
Second.	
Third.	

What I read so far caused me to *reconsider* the following preconceptions or preconditioning:

First.	
Second.	
Third.	

Rediscovering and Powering Your Leadership Qualifications

In rediscovering your qualifications', go back in your mind and heart to what led to or revealed your leadership abilities. Now go farther back in your life to when you noticed its qualifiers first surfacing in you. Such an exercise can help you reconnect your memories with what made you stand out in the past. It can move you to reconstruct what caused you to excel frequently in life over the years, without knowing why. If you find this difficult, you may need an independent counselor or an objective coach to guide you through the process. However, by all means, keep at it. The people that promoted you saw something exceptional in you that you may well have forgotten or downplayed amid the flurry of reactions to your promotion. Above all, don't consider quitting too soon because when things die down, and they will, all concerned will appreciate you staying in the fast. As you move from shock, awe, and dismay to stability, calm, and reason, you'll surprisingly find your inner self was absorbing and assimilating the job subconsciously as you in your mind were going through the motions. That is why you do not consider jumping ship too soon. Those abilities and attributes that brought you to the attention of your leaders performed without your awareness and kept you going when

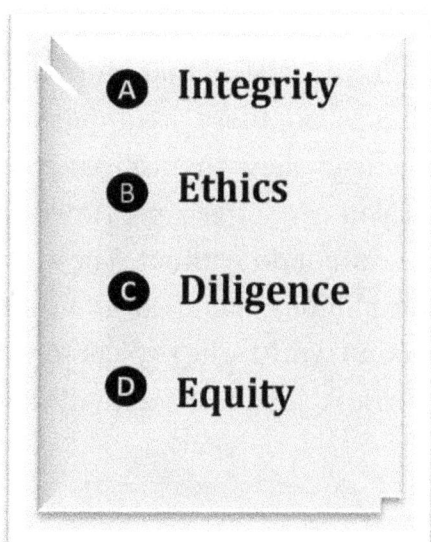

- **A** Integrity
- **B** Ethics
- **C** Diligence
- **D** Equity

you thought you were failing or floundering. How do you know this? There are at least two ways that let you know.

The first way to know is that your promoters remain pleased with you, encouraging you, even if they may have had to steer and redirect or correct you at times. The second way to know is your followers are adjusting to you. Hardly anyone is seeking to get rid of you anymore. The assaults have greatly diminished while cooperation at the same time increased. These are two sure signs, but there is a greater one than these. That is what you were promoted to do. Mysteriously, you managed to get done what you were promoted to do. Despite your sometimes, upsetting orientation process. These are all very good signs your promotion was not a mistake. Given more time, results will prove your promotion to be the best thing that could happen at this point in your life. All very good reasons not to react too hastily to your initial leadership adversity and stressors. Eventually, you get on with the business of serving your organization the way it promoted you to do, learn and refine your personal leadership style.

Leadership is So Much More Than Paperwork

Here is where things start to come together. Sooner or later, you realize that more than paperwork and supervising others is involved in leadership. While these are important, the actual definers that separated you from those you now lead show themselves apart from the reports, reviews, and other administration that you cannot escape. However, there are faculties and facilitators your leadership success cannot do without. These are what make you an impressive and effective leader. Specific abilities, qualities, and traits determine how well you manage yourself and your leadership world. They speak to you what drives your discharges and disciplines. They are fairness, justice, objectivity, and decisions.

All four stems from your character and its judgment center. What you call upon to resolve your organization's leadership issues. A unique proclivity for them was always resident in your soul and mind. They were not called upon very often in your pre-leadership life. Still, they were there and come to life when people test, your strength, and fairness as their leader. The four areas are repetitive inspectors' criticizers of your leadership tests. As dischargement[11] and disciplines, they are utilized again and again as people experience your leadership style. You will find that all sides of the issue will try you in these areas to determine and assess your leadership effects on their lives. At the outset, your testers observe and judge your reactions and resolutions through their resistance, conduct, attitudes, and behaviors. Knowing the rules or not, some will disobey them, refuse to conform, or belligerently comply (if they comply at all) with what you previously, prior to your leadership, did with them when you were on their side. Often, they will reenact antics you once liked with them and routinely ignored or exploited.

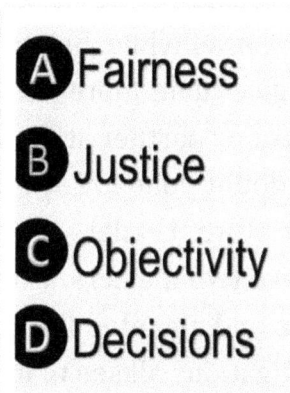

As your former coworkers' new leader, anticipate their enticements. They will entice and provoke you to see if you continue their traditions and join them or if you will discipline them for breaking rules you once snubbed. If as a new leader, you are not all that committed to your new leadership post, they have even more reason for concern. Regardless of whether you relive their antics with them or not, you are no longer one of them and in fact, are above them. The authority that comes with your position makes them vulnerable and uncomfortable to you because you know their tricks and disruptions, and that makes them quite wary of you. Normal new leader conflicts and tensions are magnified and so further obligated you to prove yourself to all parties to your promotion. Immediately, former coworker annoyances and promoter expectations demand you establish whose side you are on, even if you think you already answered the question by taking the promotion.

---

[11] Executive accomplishments to accomplish or complete, as an obligation.

Initially, former peers and pals may rejoice over your refusal to leave them behind. They may appreciate and applaud you sacrificing what you must become for what you were before the promotion. Don't lean on either because that won't last long. At the outset, they commend you and brag about how you are still their pal. Those you are to lead will do so for a brief while. But, as the weight of the position's burdens settle on you and you begin to give them more and more excuses for why you are no longer available to them as a guest or partner at their events due to work demands, they will get suspicious and start to doubt your loyalty. Here is where you find the truth in what the Lord Jesus says in Scripture. Leaders try as they might and despite keeping up appearances, no one can serve two masters. They will hate one and love the other; they will eventually cleave to one and abandon the other. That is just how life works. Timing and seasons, events and obligations all see to it. Therefore, if you fail to make the right choices concerning those you now lead, your promotion in their eyes means you changed for the organization and so they must change toward you. History and experience have shown them that the elevated you are not guaranteed to decide in their favor when they need it most, nor are you likely to carry out your new work demands to their advantage.

Time to Stop Reading and Start Acting

In preparation for assessing yourself as a leader, the following elements and components can be used as familiarization and corrective practices. Selecting and combining the following sharpens your critical thinking, situation assessment, and other leadership skills and deepens your knowledge and knowhow to prove yourself as a leader over a 120-day period.

Develop a profile to assess yourself as a leader the first 90-days. Check the boxes that apply—at least four—and proceed to create a personal assessment out of those you choose. Lay it out as a leader would and style it in a way that you can use to assess your supervisees. Select those that spoke to you most during the reading.

THEORY TO PRACTICE KNOWLEDGE TRANSFERENCE MATRIX

☐ Explore ☐ Enactment ☐ Inclination ☐ Retaining Knowledge ☐ Cases Study and Assessment ☐ Critical Thinking ☐ HK Drills ☐ Unit Content Scenarios ☐ Inspired Handling Necessary Change ☐ Dealing with Typical Leadership

Simulations ☐ Experimenting with New Ideas ☐ Applying Scripture ☐ Relating Reading to Your Position ☐ Identifying and Recognizing Appropriate Assessment Tools and Utilities. ☐ Gauging and Measuring Success ☐ Recognizing Quality ☐ Recognizing Deficiencies and Correcting Them ☐ Spotting Promising Talent and Cultivating It ☐ Getting the Floundering and Wayward Back on Track ☐ Transferring Goals and Objectives to Action ☐ Assessing Outcomes ☐ Discovering Setups, Setbacks, Shortfalls ☐ Identifying and Solving Conflicts

If you are a class or training group, compare notes, share thoughts, explain or justify selections and clarify what motivated you to take the direction, path or course of action you chose. After completing this exercise, resume your reading.

CHAPTER 13

FUNCTIONING IN YOUR NEW LEADERSHIP POSITION

To begin functioning effectively in your new position, you need to be oriented to and acquainted with another side of leadership you may know little about. The business side that plans and thinks, and governs, and decides what will or will not take place in an organization. The side that determines how things are going to happen in the business and who will be responsible for supervising them and getting them done. The side that organizes, administrates, and oversees the workings and dealings of the entity you serve. The side we are talking about is the World of Leadership. Regardless of the position you hold today, any promotion means a series of changes will, of necessity take place in your life. *Do not be deceived by the old adage that says "promotion will not change me."* As much as we would like to think so, the opposite is actually true. The demands of an elevated position, many of which are out of the leader's immediate control, means you must change. Depending on how high or sensitive your new position, you will be forced to grow. To give your best, and if your new post is critical your all; your lifestyle, past activities, and pursuits will be drastically altered in many ways. Not only is this advice needful, but it should also be heeded. You would be wise to expect the changes and to seek them out to ease your transition. Moreover, you should commit to making every prudent change, especially those that adapt to your new world. This is needful for you to prosper your new leadership post. No matter how trendy and liberating it sounds to declare in the beginning that promotion to leadership will not change you The truth is your advancement does bring (and compel) change. To keep your post and to fulfill the reasons you were appointed to it, the rapid change will sweep your life at staggering rates. Here is why.

In taking a *"Mobilizer"* I will stimulate my reading discussers with:

First.	
Second.	
Third.	

As I read through this section, the statements that inspired my implementation ideas are:

1.	
2.	
3.	

Reasons Leadership Promotion Changes Must Be

Professional changes that overflow in your world are to be expected. Smart leaders anticipate them and initiate what must be changed. Some take the lead, others get led away by them. When you take on leadership, your time becomes greatly eroded because of the increased duties and tasks put upon you. At the outset, there just will not be much left over for the many activities you are engaged in before being promoted. That is if you want to excel in your new post. If that you, then you should know anonymity is long gone. In its place, you become a conspicuous part of a wonderful machine that depends on you for its operations, safety, and profitability. Until you acclimate to your new world, you should anticipate exposure, upsets, and settling and resettling becoming routine. Anything not directly, or significantly, related to what is <u>expected</u> of you should be thoughtfully weighed against what your new role requires. What you must do, make every effort to do efficiently. Things you have probably done before, those "unmanageables" and conveniences in your life will have to be turned around as they compete for your new life role. Vain, futile, and frustrating activities (in and out) of your position will have to be carefully rearranged, discarded, or altered altogether. Instead, more pains than usual have to be taken to assure there is enough of you to go around, and that you do not burn out.

To further assure that those depending on you to shoulder your share of the work are not disappointed, daily adjustments are made. Time consciousness and sensitivity must be developed, as you prioritize everything for the sake of order and expediency. The word that best marks your transition is *expected.* You are now going to be surrounded by **expectations**; lots of them, which probably has never happened before; at least not on such a grand scale. The number of expectations, you had before may not have been at the magnitude you will be suddenly experiencing them. In the beginning, it can be said that all you will be exposed to for some time to come are EXPECTATIONS. Initially, you may find yourself resenting them until you get used to them. To not make the mistakes others that entered and exited leadership so quickly that they hardly left a mark on it made, you will have to take this counsel to heart. Launch your new leadership by valuing the trust you are given because that is what leadership intends and bestows a trust. You are in a position of trust, regardless of the office or title you hold. Suddenly, you are no longer in the background demanding, complaining, or criticizing. You are now the target of your former coworkers or peer verbal attacks. People are no longer including you in their attacks on authority, nor are you any longer part of the disgruntled responses to what they feel leadership did or failed to do for them. You are that supervisor, boss, manager, leader. You are on the other side and that too, forces change upon you. Voiced or not, people will expect you to be different no matter how much you vow to stay the same.

As a "Talk It Out" approach my reading discussion points begin with:

First. _____.
Second. _____.
Third. _____

Actionizers:

First. _____.
Second. _____.
Third. _____

Additional Reading Exercise

Draft a reading Commentary that depicts and assesses your scope of knowledge of what you gained from what you just read. Your commentary can be brief or extensive, theoretical or technical so long as it is *indisputably* tied to leadership in general and yours in particular. Your opinions and observations must be, supported by Scripture's passages that correlate with the Lord's brand and model of leadership. Be sure to give due credit for your Scripture applications and name the biblical figures you use. Lastly, but not least importantly, your commentary has to be useful. That means, it must provide a) features, b) functions, c) elements, d) components that effectively accustom and nurture new leaders' credibility. Qualitative and Quantifiable Leadership Factorates[12]

Working on Your Spiritual Wisdom and Intelligence

Some of the factors you want to consider including in your profile are:

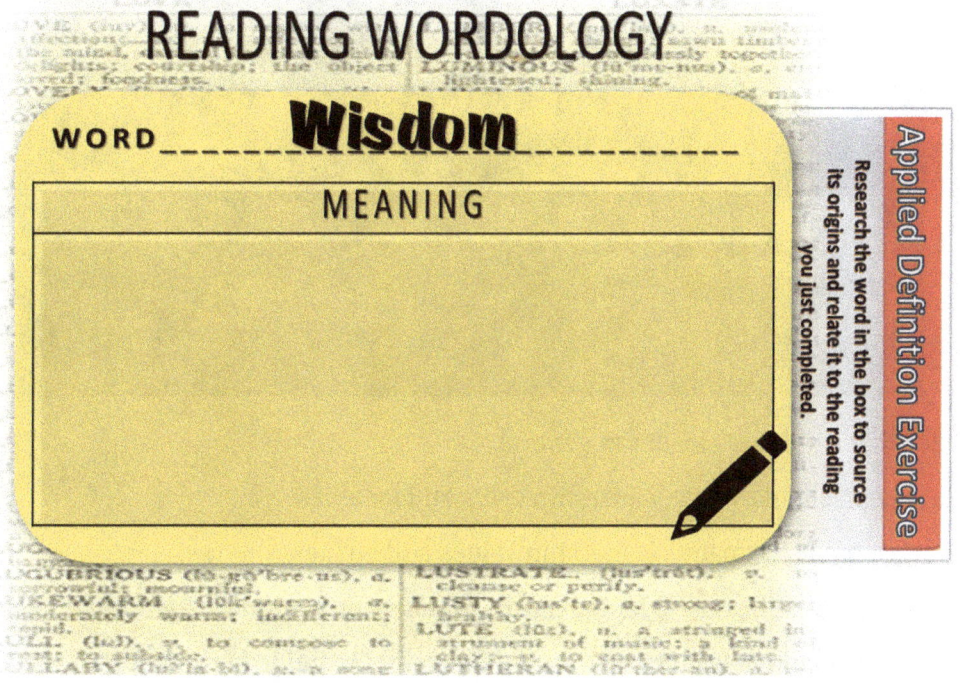

---

[12] From the word 'factor', adding the -ate at the end modifies the word to define the state and function of the noun so modified. In this instance, 'factorate' pertains to the distinctives that goes beyond identifying to specify and characterize facts used to assess or otherwise evaluate. Dr. Paula Price, PhD.

The next section lists twelve areas of leadership contemplations that you as a new leader want to give thought to as you adapt to your new leadership position. Going over them will position your mind for the transitional shifts thrust upon you as a newcomer to leadership. Visualizing and comprehending them will quicken your maturity as a developing leader and enlarge your capacity to undertake its gamut of tasks and obligations confidently, and competently. To that end, read over the statements that follow and imagine how a new leader can benefit from each one. Note what you envision to be the best way to describe and apply or relate your mental imagery to those you lead and those you share this information with professionally.

a) Visualize what validates a leader in general.
b) Articulate what should verify leadership traits and faculties.
c) Outline reasonable normative leadership values and virtues.
d) Sketch the most significant evidential marks that ingrain genuine leadership in the psyche.
e) Provide useful adaptive leadership tips and indicators to guide new leaders.
f) Specify quantifiable psycho-emotional shifts required to conform to real leader demands;
g) Enumerate relatable criterial metrics that gauge a new or prospective leader's quality and reliability.

h) Assign identifiable characteristic ethics, standards, consistency and uniformity norms

i) Exemplify the fidelities and judiciousness that symbolize stable leadership.

j) Typify the most fundamental leadership indicators.

k) Epitomize the most functional and possibly dysfunctional leadership modes.

l) Detail how new leaders can and should embody generic leadership concepts all new leaders should grasp and build upon.

Learn and Lead Exercise

Take your responses to the above and combine into an essay that profiles and articulates what you now know and expect from leadership beginning with your own. Your essay should contain 100 words and consist of the highpoints of the work you just completed. Discuss your finished product with your peers or classmates.

Inducting the Above as an Incoming Leaders

The first step in the assessment process starts with the classifiers. These demonstrate a new leader's perception of relevance. It is particularized in definable speech and deeds that display a leader's spoken and unspoken attitudes and aptitudes. The second step is examples of leadership foresight that predict (or anticipate) and prepares for common leadership eventualities and sudden developments. Such examples may be deduced from the new leader's sustained composure, especially during crises or duress. Deducements discern and extract instances of leader reactions under pressure and the effects of those actions on others, and the frequency of such outcomes. These comprise the reasons and ways a quality newcomer does well with experience gained from training, trial, and error, and supervised practice <u>before</u> being appointed to a leadership position. When they are not, new leaders are thrown into unanticipated fiery trials and intense persecution, unprepared for their impact on their world and trauma to their lives. What your readings repeatedly warn you to do as a future leader, new or elevating one is to anticipate and <u>pre</u>pare to respond properly and prudently to whatever awaits you in your new leadership post.

CHAPTER 14
CLASSIC EXPECTATIONS REQUIRED OF YOUR LEADERSHIP

In addition to the required changes, constantly you will be faced with things that <u>must be done</u> that you alone can or should do. Routinely, you will be delegated asks on top of your regular duties that must be carried out and inevitably always cannot wait. Huge time blocks should be set aside for your new duties so you must perform them promptly and satisfactorily, Many of them only you cannot handoff, but must handle them personally. Examples of such are, planning, supervising, and managing. All of which can, if you allow it, keep you emotionally, spiritually, and psychologically stretched. Free time will at first seem obsolete as meetings, conferences, and extras of all kinds (especially training extras) vie for your presence and attention. Responsibility weighs heavily upon the new leader in the young days of higher service.

The key to a successful leadership transition, however, is realization and acceptance. All newly promoted leaders must accept that life and living will dramatically differ upon leadership day one. Both are altered by the higher call and force you to yield to the unfamiliar and subsequent requirements that accompany promotion. Because of these, you may feel you are constantly in over your head. You are the "go-to" person everyone looks to for decisions and actions that you at first know little to nothing about and are yet relied on to handle. Here is where you will be grateful for your training. For if you have it, you can trust it to kick in when you need it regardless of how well you did or how aware you are of it working. Your training will tackle the hard stuff and get you through situations sometimes beneath your subconscious. That is the power of equipment, readiness, and instillation of functional principles and practices that define it, and not just installation into a position. Stepping into the world of leadership have you doing things you saw others do and wondered how they got it all done and what made them stay in the game. Now you are their equal and must compel yourself to function similarly in your new post and its seamless relentless Questions are hurled at you from the moment you enter your new office.

"Do you know anything about this? Whom do I see for that? Who is in charge of this and what am I to do next?" Behind the pressing responsibilities comes the continual and increasingly complex problem solving and the emerging issues you never noticed or heard of before are ceaseless. What you let your supervisor handle before is now thrust upon you. You are the one expected to see the most expedient courses of action to take on matters and situations you were previously oblivious to. Heads turn to you for guidance and direction. You are the wonder worker. The problem solver, the critical thinker, the solutionist and peacekeeper. You are the creative thinker, the strategist, arbitrator, and overseer of your leadership sphere. You are the check and balance, the fiscal agent, the revenue generator (or at least one of them). Mysteriously, how to make it happen and manage the demands gradually become second nature to you, if you can just survive the first nature hesitancy and insecurity attempting to drag you down. Know this, you will. Your strength and stamina will groom, your endurance with increase and your capacities will enlarge themselves with every triumph. Look for it, expect it, and realize that it is all there waiting for you to not panic but manage.

Surprisingly, the planning, organization, structure, and insight become your main concerns as you discern that in the beginning, few can help you. While it is true, these can be, and usually are, uncertain times. They will calm down. You will regain your composure and confidence and consistently meet your goals. In doing so, you fulfill your obligations and deftly tackle with ease, the overwhelming expectancies of your new world. Time to pause your reading for a while and work on the next Reinforcement Activity. See it below and follow its instructions or actions.

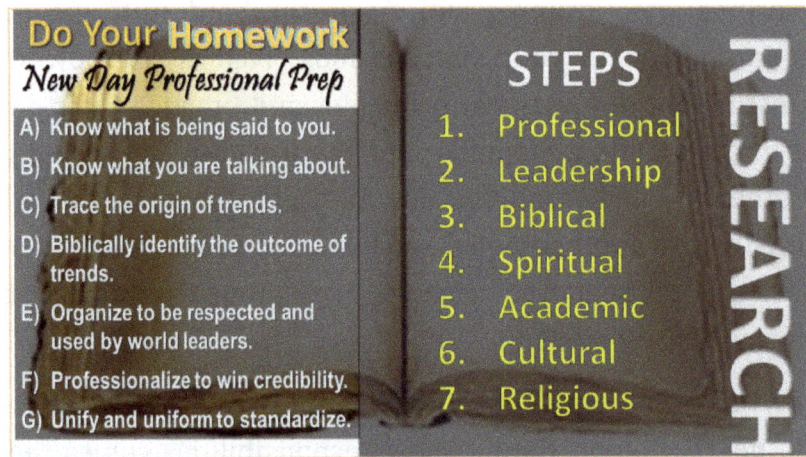

As a "Write It Out" my completed reading my summarization points begin with:

First.	
Second.	
Third.	

Illustrators: Depict how each one will look when you implement it as part of your reading's visualization and enactment. When you are finished, resume your reading with the next section.

1.	
2.	
3.	

New Leader Shocks & Wake Ups

Your promotion to leadership, day by day turns you into another person consciously or not. You may not want to admit it and your old acquaintances may choose to ignore it. But, in reality, who you were before your promotion will steadily give way to the characterizations of your new sphere of the domain. Actually, what you really become is not a new individual, but a manifestation of the one that was locked inside you all your life. The more you dive into your new world and rise to its demands, the more your old self surrenders to the buried leader in you. Originally, before your promotion, you only exhibited the traits and actions of a leader when called upon to take charge of something. Outside of that, you hardly knew they were there. This happened because the hidden leader in you and its attributes was already stashed within you. The barrier preventing their previous appearance, you now or will realize, was not having a reason to call on and employ them before. As a result, they remained inactive or only partially (or occasionally) used. Which is why you only saw them as temporary and not constant and so hesitated to call yourself a leader. Lack of opportunity restricted their on-demand availability and your cultivation of their strengths. So, when people begin to accuse you of changing because of your promotion, don't argue with them because on a primitive level, they're right. The difference is, what they call, *change* is really *unveiling*.

Take an *actionizing* break and respond to the following. If you are a class or training group, compare notes after completing to encourage and enlighten each other on prudently using what you learned so far. Share responses to critique them plus and minus, and then collaborate on the best responses and how valuable they could be as qualifiers, benchmarks, criteria, and metrics. Once the interactions related to the assignment are done, resume your readings.

As a "Talk It Out" approach my reading discussion points begin with:

First.	
Second.	
Third.	

As I read through this section, the statements that inspired my implementation ideas are:

1. _____
2. _____
3. _____

Stop here and develop scenarios or simulations for what you just wrote and roleplay it with your peers, colleagues, friends, and family. Take some time to discuss the actions and results as a group afterward. Then resume your reading.

CHAPTER 15
THE HUMAN CAPITAL 'C' SUITE

To understand this concept, take people skills for instance. As a leader, you need exceptional <u>people-insight</u> and <u>human instincts.</u> Of all the matters and issues that make pair indispensable is their value and validity to the leadership spectrum. The two will no doubt be your greatest resource. Consider them your viability and profitability instruments. Never see a single person in your position is worthless. It may be they cannot deliver for you, are misplaced, or too underdeveloped for you to see their greatness, and every creature has the greatness to be harvested by the right leader. Nonetheless, perceptive leaders know every person that crosses their path has something worthwhile to offer just waiting for their skills to discover it. No one on the planet is without some quality inborn and inbred complex of assets that make them useful to the rest of the world. Talent worthiness is why they are called human capital. The wealth of the human capital 'C' suite is the beginning of every person's and every entity's economy. When nurtured and employed, they create and increase the treasury that finances their earthly existence. The entire world relies on people's Human 'C' Suite's Wisdom Pack. The Almighty supplied every one of His creatures with

one. So what is this Pack you ask? It is an amalgamation of ten qualities and aptitudes that insert tradable capital to your life. The substance of your Wisdom Pack is what you trade for money to live on and thrive. Following is a list of the ten Q&A's of your human 'C' suite.

The Wisdom Pack Consists of:

> Attach one of each of these to the list of wisdom pack attributes below.
> 1) how to think it; 2) how to recognize it; 3) how to use it; 4) how to act on it) and how to impart its wisdom to others.

1. **Gifts** – Inborn or inbred naturalities that empower and facilitate skillfulness.

2. **Talents** – Weighted inclinations and dispositions that turn desire into person revenue.

3. **Endowments** -- Creator apportioned capacities and capabilities to finance earthly existence.

4. **Enduement** – Power doctrinally invest inherent and innate gifts, talents, and faculties with due drive, passion, and motivation

5. **Education** – Imparted information that instills knowledge, wisdom, and knowhow to function or perform.

6. **Experience** – Observational, experimental, trial and error sampling of knowledge or knacks to test and prove its validity and reliability so as to become competent at using it.

7. **Expertise** – Wisdom gained through experience, acquiring special knowledge expanded by extensive practice and experience that makes one an authority on its depth and breadth of skill and spans of appliability.

8. **Potencies** – Innate or cultivated abilities and capabilities that make one a master, especially as overcoming obstacles and achieving the impossible through an endowment of unique might (mental or physical).

9. **Powers** – Ability to act, do, perform efficaciously, mightily, potently, and authoritatively to achieve, attain, or conquer.

10. **Faculties** – Particular and performable mental or physical properties that enable functions, operations, skills and creation of opportunities for learning, accomplishing, and accumulating prosperity: engenders wisdom to obtain wealth.

Follow Up Reinforcement

Action Recommendation: As a "Talk It Out" approach my reading's conversational points begin with:

First. _____.
Second. _____.
Third. _____.

As a "Write It Out" my completed reading my summarization points begin with:

First. _____.
Second. _____.
Third. _____.

Wisdom Pack Observations Task

Describe 2 reflections the reading inspired. Say how each one relates to your entrance into the world of leadership in general and the particular level an area of leadrship you are appointed.

Envision how you would use what you just learned to upgrade your leadership service enhanced by readings and its relevance to where you are in the leader spectrum.

Following your **Reflection** assignment, draft a reading Commentary that depicts and assesses your perceptions and reactions of most recent reading. Your commentary should be substantive and present your theories, technical approaches, or your theoretical perspectives for future lessons. so long as it is *indisputably* tied to leadership and amplifies what may be obtained from the ten meanings given above. You want to relate them your leadership in particular. Your opinions, conclusions, and observations must be supported by correlating Scripture passages that align with the Lord's brand and model of leadership. Be sure to give due credit for your Scripture applications and name the biblical figures you use your work. Lastly, but not least importantly, your commentary has to be useful. That means, it must provide practical elements and conclusions that effectively orientate and develop a new leader's credibility.

Some of the factors you may want to consider putting into your profile are how the ten definitions clarify a leader; articulate quality leadership traits and faculties, classic leadership criteria and metrics allude to leadership concepts all new leaders should adopt.

Awakened Latent Leadership Talents Affirm Destiny

The latent skillsets that predestined you to be a leader eventually become remarkable, providing you with intelligence and acumen that manifest outwardly as wisdoms you scarcely knew were there. But God knew they were there, He endowed you with them for leading others when the time came for you to do so. All your life on the way to becoming a born learner or and astutely trainable one, the Lord coaxed and coached you to this point in your life. Although you may not be aware of all that is resident in you to fulfill your post and carry out its  duties, your new role will surface and convey these to you. They will provide you with what you need when and as you need it over time. You can count on them as your "Human Capital 'C' Suite" of capacities and capabilities that supply your leadership self with brilliance and pragmaticism.

Leaders are More Than Mechanics

Leadership is more than mechanics or mechanisms, and leaders are more than human machines, robots. These are why psychology, humanities, and similar disciplines are included in quality readiness programs. They allow you to build people in ways that motivate them to protect the work of your position. Furthermore, the critical people insight such disciplines impart expands your capacity to motivate and strengthen those under you. When employed keenly, people knowledge acquired from mere cursory exposure to these fields reveals what workers and supporters to respond best. Understanding human nature keeps leaders from under, valuing them and instead motivates them to prosper and benefit whoever elevated you to leadership. At important times, your people instincts will prompt and instruct you on what it takes for you to incessantly develop those in your charge. Remember the best of you is only profitable when you pass it on to others in ways that bring out the best in them. Keep that thought in mind and permit it to germinate (and ruminate) peak leadership attributes in you.

Rarely stressed in many leadership settings or training is the underlying potency of authentic leaders. Preeminently, leaders are teachers. Be they human resource instructors, departmental supervisors, various levels of management. Leaders are teachers and they should be because most of what they do in their day involves educating, cultivating and refining. For example, in one way or another, a leader will have to take on and informatory role. Here are a few ways those who lead invariably fall into a teaching mode outside a classroom:

- answer questions,
- clarify the answers,
- instruct workers on what to do and how to do it, and
- advise then on the how to get the best our of their service or employment.

True leaders are innate teachers and natural guardians. They guide people to the knowledge and intelligence that prosper their lives and livelihoods. With that, they further guard people and their work so success is more frequent than failure. Quality leaders make up a major part of the organization's hedge of protection. Scarcely an hour, not to mention a day, goes by when a leader is not engaged in some teaching instance to inform and clarify something to their workers and staff. A fact that makes leaders mainly teachers, perhaps before they settle into their managerial or supervisory roles. Most people view leadership as bossing or commanding and that is true. But between these two actions is the constant called teaching. Teaching is so embedded in leadership that most leaders dismiss that ongoing part of their functions. Few of them stop and think, "I instruct more than I command. I educate more than I supervise. I train more than I steer my subordinates. I explain more than I discipline or correct." If they did, they would wonder when and how did it get that way. After a while, they will realize the importance of reading their position's materials, guidebooks, manuals, and routine correspondence. Doing so assures what they dispense to their people is timely and accurate.

Becoming a Leader Right Away

When you become a leader, you are immediately expected to protect your organization's prospects, potentials, opportunities, supplements, properties, standards, and protocol. These necessities include but are not limited to your duty to what is listed below. As an activity, state what each one says or means to you in one sentence.

a) comfort: _____

b) coach: _____

c) coax: _____

d) monitor: _____

e) supervise: _____

f) see to: _____

g) nurture: _____

h) develop: _____

i) instruct: _____

j) discipline: _____

k) guidance: _____

l) counsel: _____

Twelve specific conducts those who promoted you want to witness in effect as part of your promotive agreement with them. And, they want to see them active and operative right away. Complying with their expected benefits your entity's existence and also enhances and fortifies them as a force. In this respect, your existence as a leader counteracts whatever impedes your entity's progress. Diligences in these areas stops their neglect from jeopardizing its existence or hindering its prosperity. The guardianship aspect of your leadership curtails infamy, backlash, and various negative reactions and initiatives waged against your assigned organization. As you can see procedural and protocolic mechanics are a fraction of what you as a leader does.

To do your job well, your perception of life, the people you lead, and those who ordained you must all change. Former disparagements, snubbery, and above all favoritism that ranks your team according to your personal idealism and ideologies and not by their performance or potential pigeon holes them. Those you like are advantaged before and usually above those that strike no symbiotic chords with you. To recognize when you fall into bias traps, look at it this way. Examine your leadership ways. Which of your team comes to mind first when you think of or must appoint one of them to do anything? How often is the same person sought and selected? Is the one you turn to most frequently the best person for the job or the most compatible with you? How about notifications? Who do you consistently leave out; that is, forget to notify when you spread information your group or department needs? Are you constantly apologizing to so and so for overlooking them again, or neglecting to provide them with news and data the others get readily? If you, you should check your bias meter. Whom do you fail to invite to group outings or just lunch with the leader? How many times do those you find yourself incognizant of stumble upon you associating with your favorites or discussing some fun time you had with them? It is important that you check your leadership prerogatives and preferences in these areas because actions like these do more than hurt feelings. They breed impartiality that denies viable candidates for prestigious posts and assignments opportunities to compete or to be taken seriously. Human nature being innately prone to its comfort and pleasures subtly satisfy both by inclining those in power and position to offload the burden of camaraderie self about the Fairness and fair play in decisions, selections, work responsibilities, division of duties and tasks should all be a matter of course for your leadership style. The reason is, your acceptance of a leadership position means you covenant with your leaders to observe and practice things from the vantage point of one chosen to uphold their entity's standing with God. And in addition to this, right standing within its community.

CHAPTER 16
BUSINESS & ENTREPRENEURSHIP EQUAL COVENANT

Remember your entity has a business and entrepreneurial covenant with its community. However unspoken or undeclared it may be, there is nonetheless an implied contract based on trading transactions. In exchange for their currency, customers, consumers, and clients[13] all receive a particular product sold to them or a performed service. For their patronage, they receive respect, quality, and service. Proprietor credibility depends on a business' reliability. That means, the business opens on time, carries quality merchandise or delivers exceptional service, and consumers are treated justly. Difficulties are resolved quickly, reparations and compensations, if they are due are acknowledged and swiftly remitted. Consequently, according to what's been said, new leaders must cooperate with their entity's credentialers. In this vein, you too should be as concerned with your organization's proper standing in the community and its fiscal soundness as the entity itself. Both depend on the potency of its leaders and laborers as much as business traffic and revenue.

---

[13] Buyers, users, recipients.

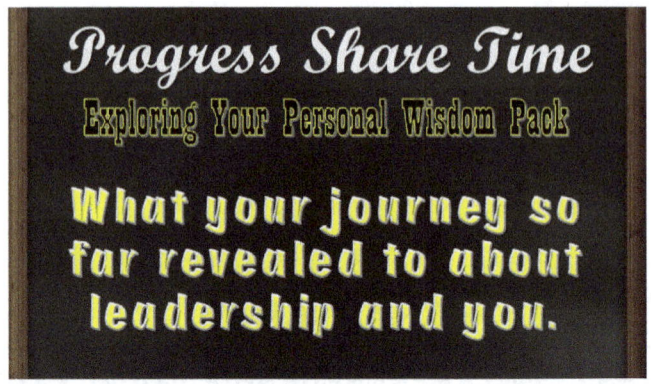

Succumbing to Requisite Leadership Changes

Compelled attitude changes and mental perspectives, should not be hindered or restrained. They should be respected and thus allowed to transform you. If not, you will drop your guard, flail in your service, and frustrate more than you mitigate. How you speak to people, how you present yourself, and interact with those you lead are of utmost importance for all of these reasons. New leaders more than the others, must start out positive and not timid. From day one they must be upbeat about their post and those they lead. To set the right tone, new leaders ought to be decisive and caring from the start. These measures tend to ease people and create a productive and enthusiastic work climate. Remember, morale is pivotal to good leadership and strong cooperation. Low morale emotionally recommends departure. High morale encourages entrenchment. People want to be happy. They want to feel good about their jobs. And, they prefer and cooperate with leaders that appreciate these two aspirations. A word of caution though. Always remain cognizant of one potential misconstrual as a leader. While it is helpful to listen to their "feel goods" make sure that they are not using them as a ploy to avoid giving their all or to fall short in their performances. It is a mistake to give the impression that worker contentment takes precedence over paying customers and satisfied employers or investors. Doing so imperceptibly tells both parties the come and go, staff, carries more weight in the matter than those patronizing the business or supporting the venture. Workers should know that what keeps the entity viable and profitable is not their favorite this or that: What actually keeps the doors open and the traffic streaming into the establishment. Consumers and clients are a concealment bunch. They want peace, and they want comfort. So they most likely will not tell you they are unhappy about something disturbing about your entity. Instead, most just drift away without ever giving a chance to address the matter. Be sure the lines between worker comfort and customer satisfaction are not blurred.

As a leader, you should let your people know that they are on your premises or with you to work. That is, to produce a product; make sales, handle business. And as a priority, to please customers and clients as much as you can. Workers and staff should also know that in the spirit of fairness and objectivity, you have their back when difficulty arises against them. They serve assured you will prudently investigate matters before accusing or censuring them when critics and resenters mobilize against you. Or, should you render unpopular decisions that yield unfavorable outcomes, or distress workers by unduly (in their minds) that overwhelms them? Appreciation should be typical of your leadership style. Those who do well should know it because recognizing good work and service inspires hope in onlookers secretly desiring to be honored for their efforts too.

Be Different to Become Exceptional

Exceptionality has almost become a bygone objective in today's laxity. A great deal of degradation has gone into making the indifferent and the lackadaisical content with doing what they deem to be their best. So pervasive is this attitude that customer service and satisfaction are disparaged as too burdensome for some entity's resources. People aiming for excellence and exceptionality are often ridiculed and chided; scorned as too serious or accused of being grovelers. Nonetheless, leaders that tend toward innovation, ingenuity, and unusualness become exceptional. Not getting locked into the norms of your position causes people to take notice of you and your work. When things are varied for good reason, people are inspired and oddly it sparks hope in them. Note the phrase "for good reason."

Varying the way things are done for no prudent reason other than to attract attention or to stand out for personal accolades can backfire. Make sure you study situations before you alter their norms. Conduct surveys, observe what is or is not working. Meaning by this that which is productive, effective, protective and profitable. Before shifting staff, focus on who is doing what and what is done by one person better than another. Avoid being hasty or impatient, especially when it comes to workers and followers.

For instance, followers who take more of your time and attention should not be ridiculed or threatened because of their special needs. Instead, you should move to identify their strengths and best traits to make these known to each staffer quickly. While doing so, go beyond praise and compliments, or even affirmation. Acknowledge and integrate staffers' positive strengths in their performance goals and objectives. Take the time to reference their achievements, regardless of how small or seemingly inconsequential. Link them to your required job skills, duties, and responsibilities to stimulate workers cooperation with your designated development plan. Positivity in all respects should be the byword of your leadership style. It should if you desire to inspire faith and confidence in your leadership within your followers.

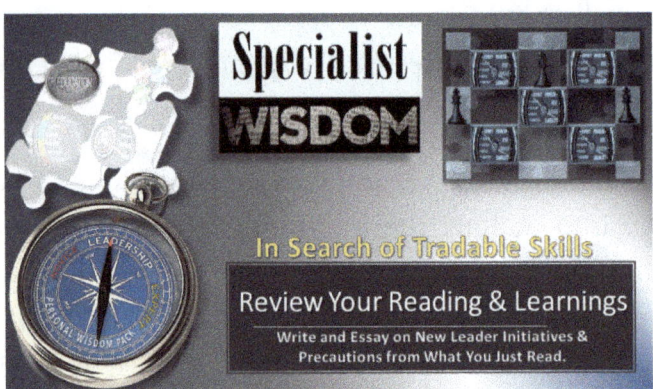

The Currency of Positivity

The word currency is most memorably associated with money, but it has other value-weighted meanings that can be applied here. For example, think of the electricity flowing in your home. Its flow is also called a current. In fact, the Online Etymology Dictionary's explanation of currency is "a condition of flowing." It means "to run", like the electricity in your house. Here is where it begins to serve our purposes. The same source adds, "state or fact of flowing from person to person." In addition, it says "continuity in public knowledge." Lastly, the money aspect enters: "that which is current as a medium of exchange, money." The money piece validates the use of the word 'tradable' on the graphic above. In respect to human capital or assets, currency attaches worth and exchange to it;

both of which happens with money. But there is more. Tradable frequents to the frequency of use, a popularity that circulates, prevalence that speaks to primacy and pervasiveness. Would you not say these effectively describe money and predominance in society? Money, says Merriam Webster is used for bartering; exchange—swapping one thing for another. The American Heritage Dictionary declares exchange, currency, and circulation go together: "Transmission from person to person as a medium of exchange; circulation." Prevalence refers to that which is, "Generally accepted for use. prevalence

Putting it all together, and positivity's meaning and its relationship to human currency surfaces. More precisely it fits the implications of the "Human Capital 'C' Suite" and its "Wisdom Pack". The flow between them is what is tradable[14]. The terms below all make the connection between your abilities and talents. The exchanges between them answer how currency relates to your tradability. Here is an example of your tradability. Exchanging your abilities for tradable currency.

You apply for a job or position. The first thing you receive in order to be seriously considered is an application. You fill it out and it earns you an interview. During the interview what you wrote on the application is discussed and its veracity confirmed. Upon being satisfied that you can do what you say and that you know what you know to meet their needs, you get a job offer. The offer comes with a salary proposition. This is where what we have been discussing enters. The amount offered in exchange for your skills and services correlates with two things. The first is the company is offering what they feel the position you are applying for is worth. The second is, the offer may or may not be what you want to trade your human capital for in their service. At this juncture, you both have the opportunity to decide your "capability currency". Ordinarily, people take jobs, or not, based on their material needs; not so much on their employable worth in respect to what a firm wants to pay them. As a leader, you will have regular occasion to assess people's "work worth". A positive self-image and view of those you lead will convince you to deal fairly with employable talents and to treat them well in their service to you.

---

[14] Countertrade, transferable, marketable, exchangeable, negotiable, saleable; buyable, exportable, acquirable, sellable; cashable and utilize.

Maintaining an attitude and conduct of positivity goes a long way toward winning trust, favor, and compliance. Positivity in this instance does not intend groundless optimism or wishful thinking. Real positivity should rest on positive opinions, feedback, and judgments that result from careful research, judiciousness, good decision-making skills, and quantifiable methodologies. The major ingredients of positivity are enthusiasm and encouragement. Be aware though that both they and positivity overall are best tempered by discretion, so as not to mislead those led or served by inspiring false hope. Excessive and ungrounded (or unfounded) positivity can breed disillusionment in those misinterpreting what you convey with your positivity. Yes, you should remain upbeat, but not when situations call for sobriety, solemnity, and truth. It is no substitute for honesty or candid assessment of situations and their obviousness. As a leader, your fundamental aim in all this is to minimize deep-rooted fears, doubts, and anxieties from your staff, especially as a newly promoted leader. Definite steps should be taken to galvanize and not intimidate your new staff. Leaders who need their people fearful and anxious, insecure themselves, their abilities, or their standing with you are people *demolishers* and not people builders. Such leaders' primary concept of leading is the destruction of the weak and not renovation of the broken.

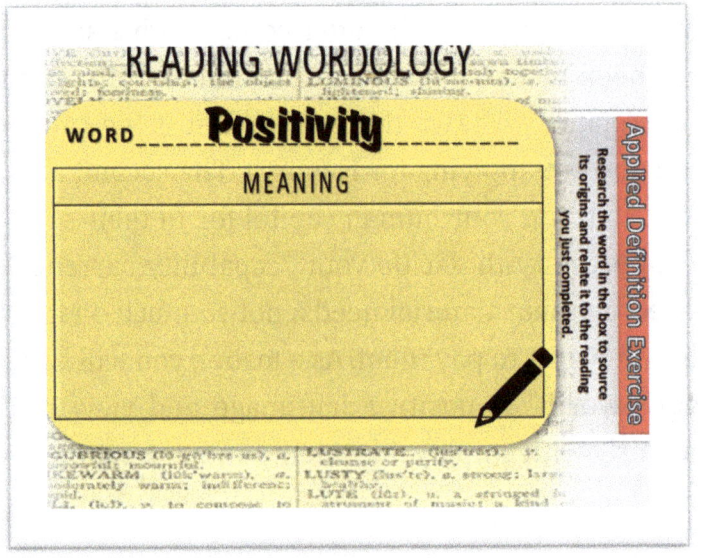

Depending upon what you as a leader are called to achieve for your organization or its departments, staff treatment can work to your advantage or disadvantage. Whichever it turns out to be, you should be circumspect in your initiatives and replies. Be sure of how your outcomes will best serve you and your business in the end before you embrace a particular leadership style as your own. Whatever your goals, grace, and thoughtfulness must permeate your leadership mentality and modes. Worker strength and sincerity should influence you as a leader if you are to cultivate obliged honest concern for people. Doing so is more than a must; it is good practice. People need to know their leaders care about them and their lives beyond their value to the entity and its endeavors. A sense of safety and security should be fostered in them that can be felt in your presence. Confidence in your leadership direction out to also be nurtured. Make your staff a welcome part of your leadership sphere without being too fraternizing. They should not be made to feel like unwanted intrusions in your leadership except when <u>you</u> need <u>their</u> service. Your staff should be tutored to partner with you, at least so far as their part in a task or project goes. Above all, they should be encouraged to believe in themselves and allowed to experience what it is like to be a teamer and not a slave.

New Leader Wake Up Stunners

To minimize shocks and upsets, new leaders should nurture their family and friends. Let them know that the change though necessary does not have to mean the deterioration of your relationship with them. Sell your beloveds on ideas and techniques that make for a peaceful transition. Enlist their help in making it work. When it comes to friends though, do not be offended when some of them choose to distance themselves. That too is part of the cost elevated new leaders must count and account for in their new lives. However, they should avoid giving the impression that their close ones' frustration and confusion are signs that they should not answer their calling. Instead, it is best to work with them to allay exaggerated fears and forge tighter bonds. Destroy vain imaginations by immediately opening and keeping open positive lines of communications. Determine to create a different yet sturdier bridge for relations with the people you love and need. Leaders' loved ones do not have to fall prey to the stereotypes that terrorize those moving up in the world. Up and comers do not have to lose his children sin, their spouse to divorce, or friendships to resentment. New leaders can patiently work through all of these customary threats to bring about a better outcome. While some drawbacks are unavoidable, everyone does not have to fear losing it all.

With all else that has been said, there is the matter of those promotionary[15] shocks associated with your rise. Pressure, pressure, pressure is heaped upon you. Accordingly, your time, once mainly your own, shrinks daily. Whatever spare time or indifferent service you once enjoyed at your convenience is absorbed by your new position and your organization. Absences and declined invitations that went unnoticed before becomes glaringly obvious. Whereas these were previously acknowledged as your privilege, now is vigorously questioned. You are now on staff and the rules are different. You are told when to come and leave and what to do while you are on duty. The organization unsympathetically assigns time-consuming tasks and appointments you formerly opted to forego. As an established entity, they periodically disinterested and unmoved by what you have planned: Particularly, in dire situations or times of urgency. As part of an organization's leadership, you are no longer entirely your own. Steadily, you alter your entire existence to fulfill sometimes impossible obligations. Extremely frustrating at the outset everything you do appears to be for everyone else but you.

At first, this may be and probably is, somewhat true. But be patient and persevere; things will quiet down as your unknown hidden leadership treasures kick-in to rescue and empower you task by task by task. You can count on this happening because your inner leader will rise to every occasion simply because you impel it. It happens by virtue of official appointment to leadership. Before then, you may recall past successes when you got people to believe in you; to trust your abilities and evidence that trust by accepting and following your guidance and advice. Other remembrances can be of you being arbitrarily chosen to lead a group or team just because...and you performed quite well every time. These recollections tend to surface on account of your promotion. It put you in charge of numerous things such as staff, resources, property, and premises. That charge made you dig deep within to draw out what would get you through the rigors of

---

[15] Promotion+ary = that which is connected to or engaged in. Of, belonging to. Hence, promotionary refers to what is connected with promotion in various contexts.

leadership as a newcomer. As an authorized or official leader, any one or all of these can be the case.

Describe 2 reflections the reading inspired. Say how each one relates to your entrance into the world of leadership in general and the particular level an area of leadership you are appointed.

Envision how you would use what you just learned to upgrade your leadership service enhanced by readings and its relevance to where you are in the leader spectrum.

Today everything is magnified regardless of any feelings of inadequacy you may experience. Despite your promotion or perhaps misunderstanding it, you may want to keep your life on the same track it's been on for years. Living a simple life concerned only about you and yours does not immediately let you go. However, taking the reins of leadership ends all of that; remaining in your shell and dismissing what is not your concern ceases almost abruptly. You were elevated because you, deliberately or subconsciously inspire trust in people, which moves them to turn to you for many things. Your inward and outer changes cause a change in others and sometimes you effortlessly, and so successfully brought order out of disorder and excellence out of mediocrity. Whether you perceive your call that way, know that others do. They place great and sometimes unreasonable burdens on you that you must recognize and handle. If you fall prey to false humility or religious piety, you will underestimate what people seek from you, and fail to deliver when it is readily within your power to do so. At times sheer fatigue, overwhelmingness can make you short-tempered and too irritated to take some requests and demands seriously enough to tackle them. You should work to prevent this from overtaking you. It can cost you greatly at the most inopportune times.

Earning Trust and Sustaining It

As the early fires of adaptation wanes, the climate around you will change. Peace will replace turbulence and trust will replace wariness. Those who meet and greet the seasoned you in your new position take for granted you worked out your integrity, stability, accountability and commitment issues. They, by virtue of what it means for one to occupy your delegated leadership position, believe you can now help them to do the same. People will see you like the model they can follow. Your endurance paid off and inspires hope in them. They approve you by trying harder and make the effort to stretch beyond their normal limits. At first, because of your leadership and later due to the fortification they gained from pressing beyond. It won't take them long to realize your leadership produced in them what they hoped. Your persistence motivated them to work hard to get over themselves and really trust what they've done alongside you. Remarkably, your inner feelings of inadequacy and unworthiness rarely expose themselves to your followers as much as you think they do. Your team only knows you get it done and make them feel good about laboring beside you.

The emotional will decrees and commands the volitional will.

Outwardly, what the Lord hid in you to lead others in the future and expertly govern His populations equip you to manage. Skillfulness in these areas is all people want to see. Unless you give them a reason to focus on your negative traits, they most often dismiss them as growth areas. Apart from that, followers tend to be comfortable or acquiesce and give you the benefit of the doubt, being okay with accepting your strengths and how you use them to overcome their weaknesses. The idiosyncrasies that you believe disqualify you from effective leadership service, most people often disregard, for your followers to choose not to give you the benefit of the doubt and opt to think the best instead of the worst of you forces them to conclude you shouldn't be their leader. As a rule, most workers prefer not to consider such a thing because it opens a host of conflicts and contradictions they would just as soon avoid. To keep their own emotional confusion and unsettledness down, they would rather trust that whoever placed you in leadership did that work for them and all they need to do is follow your lead. An attitude that prevails among those who have no hidden agenda or aspirations of rivaling you for your position.

Guardianship Guidance

As new leaders undertake this monumental yet worthwhile task, they must cover every aspect of their daily existence potentially affected by their promotion. They have to plan alternatives to what is normal so that routines will not suffer because of what is to be. Here is where newcomers can put those conciliatory and negotiation talents of theirs to work. It is beneficial to make it everyone in the household's duty to work out the new life plan to improve and preserve the family's quality of life. Ask for suggestions and use the event to upgrade the household's critical thinking and problem-solving. Create role-plays, simulations, games and cases for the household to work out to decide what will work and what cannot. Begin with a list of what is most important to every member and start the negotiation process of deciding what each person can or cannot live with, or is not willing to let go. The entire ordeal will take time, so new leaders should not rush it. Keep records and notes of troublesome issues to tackle later. Note as well the answers and approaches the family agrees to and use it as a basis to form the household's pledge of commitment their success when or after promotion comes alive and takes its place in their world. Leaders should do all that they can to make the transition a non-stressful procedure. Call time outs and reschedule sessions when inflammatory matters flare-up and refuse to be settled. Spend huge amounts of time in prayer and lead the family into a potent prayer routine as well to reduce frustrations and expedite the process.

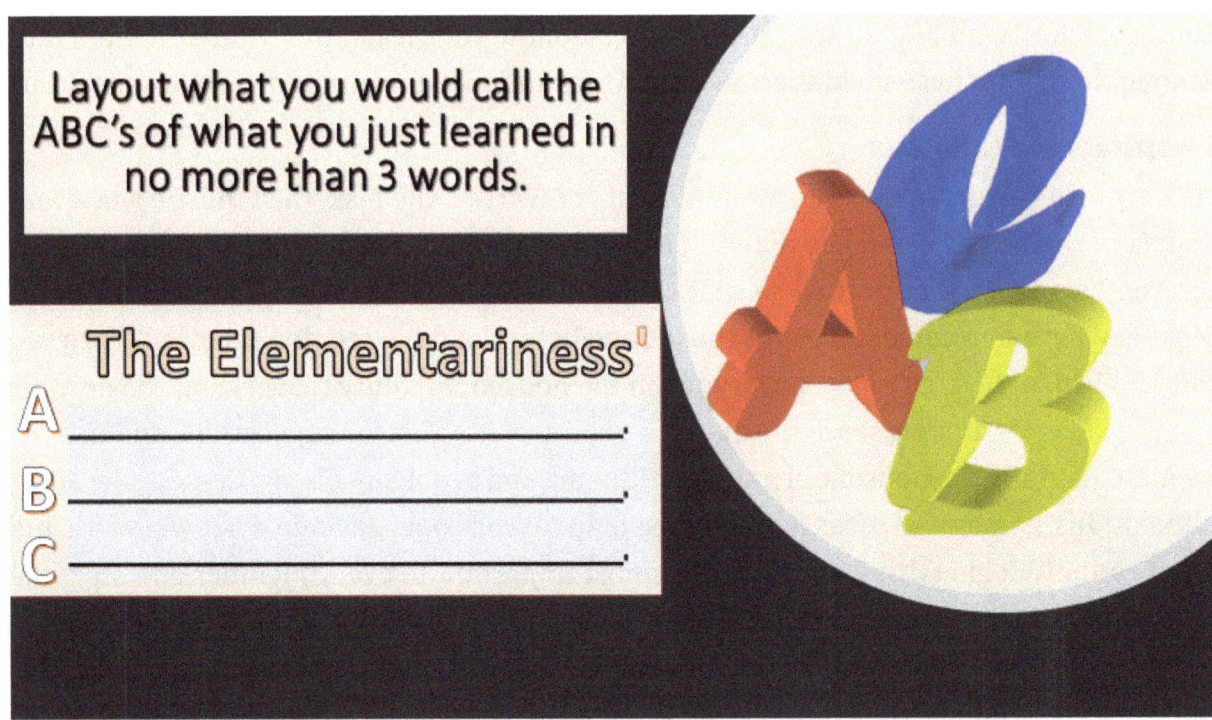

CHAPTER 17
PERSONAL LEADER SELF-REGULATION ADVICE

A significant amount of information has been shared with you throughout this tutorial. Every bit of it is useful to you as a new leader being fitted (and perhaps outfitted) for the world of leadership. A world that goes all the way back to before time and earth began and will continue throughout eternity. That means you are becoming part of an endless avocation that long ago tested and proved itself. Over eons, it developed and perfected its rules, guidelines, principles, and practices to sustain itself and operate in a multiplicity of ways. You should realize the leadership world you are entering, better yet the place you are entering may be considered a sphere on earth, but its point of origin is a realm. A realm with age-old and endless populations and eternal citizens that have been governed and guided by their respective leaders' modes before earth and time began. All this is to impress upon you that leadership descends from above and does not rise up from the earth, which is why its inhabitants come into the world needing to be led and needing leaders to lead them throughout their lives. Concluding this tutorial is your final and most impelling takeaway. That leadership operates on parameters you must thoroughly conform to in your spirit, your heart, your soul and your mind. Nothing less than total assimilation of what created and sustains the world in which you live and will serve more assures your success. There is a long list of before earth guidelines and regulations for those taking responsibility for human populations and their discrete groups. Why is it important for new leaders to know this, you ask? The answer is what this tutorial was all about, which is the adaptive changes those new to leadership must make to achieve the aims and objectives their appointers expect from them.

Adaptive changes are more than mere shifts of culture, mindsets, positions, or attitudes. They are changes of adjustments that fit a particular purpose intended to be joined to what precedes them or what follows or calibrates the adjustments. The word adaptive as used here includes the aptness that fits someone or something for circumstantial purposes by modification. Think about it. Changes that shift merely relocate, figuratively or actually. Any adjustments needed are limited to placement. Fitting or fitting in is only matters of space and measurement. These are only a small part of what adaptive changes mean. Adaptive is a more dynamically expansive term that adds constitution, substance, ability and capacity, and similar thoughts to its intents. Add that to the well-understood meanings of change and what sets it apart becomes clear. Principally, adaptation speaks to fitting change, interconnective change, adjusted or adjustable change. Thus, fitness is the key to adaptation. For the new leader, this means fit for duty, fitting in, and fitfulness of skills and abilities to be used in the position.

Fill in some adapt to leadership terms that come to mind from what you learned so far.

About Adaptive Changes

Adaptive Changes are root focused. With respect to your promotion, changes go to the root and the heart of what you bring to the leadership spectrum. The term suggests how willing you are to adapt—fit—all of you to the demands of the position you enter as a leader. If you have been paying attention to the readings, you have mostly penetrated its reasons for the activities and exercises you completed. You know by now the type ad scope of leadership changes you must make to become an effective leader. What you may not yet perceive it that they are <u>not</u> automatic. For the changes that condition and position for potent leadership to happen, you must deliberately decide to make them.

Application: Earlier the need for adaptation was discussed. Reasons for it were given to impress upon the new leader how vital it is to success and followers' recognition of your new role in their existence. One of the ways to demonstrate this is by *internalizing* what others before you in the position did, noting how it was done correctly and ways that it was not. Conformance guidelines should be <u>technologized</u> by those entering leadership followed by illustrations of success and failure. When you have completed this exercise, resume your reading.

To continue, it is a matter of record by now that change is not natural for humans. Only a few creatures adapt to their environments easily or quickly. Humans as with all the other creatures are hardwired to protect their inward and outward selves. A multiplexic[16] constitution compels them to be. Humanity's vitality relies on essentia that preserve and protect their inner, median, and outer structures. Countless materials and substances within them are designed (and designated) to guard human beings, keeping them safe and functional. A multiplex of complements[17] that are innate to core compound synthesizers[18] integrate natural and inbred regulations to secure, and when needed,

---

[16] Etymologically: "having to do with, having the nature of, being, made of, caused by, similar to. From the Greek *-ikos* "in the manner of; pertaining to", OED. *In respect to the word 'multiplexic' this etymology identifies a manifold complex born out of or emerging as a result or consequence of nature, creation, manufacture or handiwork, or cause. That which is 'multiplexic' is the product of or relevant to intrinsic actions cause by or similar to a force or agent.* The Author.

[17] Completers, suppliers, balancers, accompaniers, counterparts, harmonizers.

[18] Producers, manufacturers, creators, makers, fusers, blenders, combiners, integrators.

restore people's internal stasis[19]. Comprehensive elements frame and schedule their being's operatives to supply and maintain them as healthily as sustainable for them in their world. These same forces and factors help people recuperate from debilitating blows that damage them as swiftly as their makeup can.

New Leader Inward Checkups

As a new leader you will have to know yourself and take inventory of, not only your strengths and weakness, powers and deficits but your tendencies and reflexes as well. How your defenses, deflectors, and impulse as a rule spontaneously affects others is noteworthy. These, ought to be a matter of record to you by now fitting the categories of habit, practice, pattern, and norms. Take time to explore these in the early days of your leadership and note them in a journal to identify what works and isolate it from what has historically worked against you.

Now the reason for the closing advice. Mainly, it is to caution you against a subtle but defeating trip-up leaders in general, encounter and new leaders, in particular, should be wary of as newcomers to leadership's sphere. The trip-up in question is called in this material, "The Triple V Competence Effect." It discloses the disorders and dysfunctions of emotional competency or the lack of it. The habit of performing well or performing poorly depending upon what happens in personal life. Following is a brief explanation of this penchant.

> **Volitional Tenacity**
>
> The innate power of your will to persevere, pushback, refuse to surrender to obstacles that impede its determined success.

Variable Versus Volitional Competence

Triple V Competence a phrased coined to label disparate leadership performance results. It characterizes the attitudes that define how duties and responsibilities are undertaken and achieved, particularly during periods of hardship. It is when the emotional self decides to downgrade performance efforts or randomize their competencies whenever unpleasant or disturbing situations take place. Triple V trip-ups emerge when people in

---

[19] Balancers, stabilizers, calmers, copers, quieters,

the process of carrying out their tasks fluctuate how they use their capabilities. They exert more on good days and less on bad ones according to internal rules that regulate their volitional response to external incidents that occur in their lives. Triple V Competence is encoded in people's enactment commands from childhood and is strengthened as they mature. Deep-seated resolve set in motion applies submerged remedies to what unsettled them as youngsters to reminiscent occurrences in adulthood. Hidden from their conscious self, the remedies that served them well grew up in their character and formed their life perspectives. Over time, issue after issue built an instinctual system to determine how they impulsively overcome obstacles and recover from setbacks. Survival, revival and thrival, three perseverance impellers are called upon to rescue and boost the will's tenacity to press through difficulty and perform well in spite of it. The three also at the same time supply rationale and motives for doing so as well. Compliance with these pushers' rest with the volitional will; that aspect of human liberty and perspective on duty that deems something worthy of effort and persistence. Mustering this psycho-emotional confluence[20], a person gets (or in the past, got) through difficult demands on their talents.

Volitional Tenacity, the sheer doggedness of the character sourced by the will shore up their capabilities and propelled them to do so. Infrastructurally, the soul's core foundational supports come up to draw the emotions away from inertia and purposefully into volitional action. Which of the three it mobilizes at any given time or in what instance is where Triple V takes hold.

Depending on the infrastructure of the emotional the human will once, forged by the circumstances that affected the soul and permeated the heart, one of the three is actionized to select which one would treat and settle the effect of occurrences on the soul's resources. Typically, desire outweighs necessity and obligation. That is the basic decider that chooses which one of the three the will succumbs to the emotions whenever experienced situations contradict or clash with emotional issues. Usually, unbeknown to the leader inward exists an internal repository of human will set of reactors and responders assigned to go to work calming and confirming a person whose capabilities

---

[20] Convergence, union, inflow, influx, merger, conjunction, unification, aggregation, combination, concurrence, synchronism.

are superior until something disturbs their inner peace. When this happens the person's emotional decrees issue orders to the volitional will based on long-standing emotional ordinances. These rules subject all else to them and affect how people handle upsets and determine if they can function well under duress. If you are a new leader, you want to be aware of this reality even if you have been incognizant of its operations in the past. Over your lifetime, you have been governed and guided by these typically subconscious determiners of your will. It could be that yours are so deeply embedded inside the secret self that you never detected their existence or function before, only their effects. Effects that you take as just your way, or merely your habits. You probably discussed them often and explained away neglect, incompetence or incapabilities according to them. For instance, you may recall saying, "I'm usually good at what I do, except when so and so happens." So and so can be the family influence, physical ailment, upsetting news, or other disturbance. In effect, you are good at what you do until "life happens." Some people go so far as to put good things on the list. For example, "When I get excited over something, I get so distracted I lose sight (or forget) what I was doing or how to do it. It takes me a while to get back to what I was doing before the exciting moment.

> In effect, I am good at what you I until… "life happens."

Taken together, the two common excuses falling into these illustrations say that you are situationally excellent and cannot be relied on for consistency due to your susceptibility to outside occurrences. As a leader, such an inclination leaves those around you in a lurch. You cannot come to work if you are upset. If you manage to show up to work, you are too distracted to do your job. Your attentions are scattered and your ability to focus is virtually nonexistent. Your staff and your superiors are at a loss for what to do. Meanwhile, to protect your position, you convince yourself that even when you are upset you can still give your best. Something your rate of productivity and output disprove.

The scenario just described is commonplace in today's professional environment. For reasons inappropriate for this discussion, mysterious forces seem bent on downgrading humanity and its capabilities. Workers and professionals are persuaded daily to succumb to fragile emotional states and use them to regulate theirs on the job or in-office performance. People are affirmed for their weakness and dysfunction. Nonetheless, organizations must pay for their selectees' very subjective, invariably biased inability to keep their word or to keep up with the work they were engaged to do. The answer to this quagmire of dysfunctionality is Triple V Competence.

People contrive and attach two streams of commands to their work ethic. The decider of the two in actual situations is the human will. It determines how the mind and body perform in what circumstances and in what context, measure and degree. The volition is the variator of one's competence. Versus is the opposer; the factor that chooses an emotional state assigned to the will's command to persevere and thereby overcome difficulties, or crumble under pressure and abandon it. Variable hangs choices and outcomes in the balance. No one knows what a day's work or service for people with Triple V Competence disorder will be like. If they are extremely talented, their work buys them extensive indulgences, the cost of which is other more stable and less talented people cover for them. Just to get the result or product their spark of excellence produces. After which, they often take off until the inner self wishes to return and honor their word. Even if the person does not actually go off the scene, their capabilities and competence do and that is the purpose of this advice. What an entity and its populations typically experience is neglect, half-heartedness, absent-mindedness, indifference, and apathy; all when combined spell sloth. The kind of sloth that misses due dates, snubs deadlines, abandons tasks, and oddly, gleefully roams the facility socializing with others who are seriously engaged in their work.

> **TRIPLE V COMPETENCE DISORDER**
> A new leader that refuses to surrender to the requisites of the call and as a result never fully delivers as appointed.

Link Adaptive Change with Triple V Competence Disorder and you have a leader that refuses to surrender to the requisites of the call and as a result never fully delivers. Such a leader reneges on their promotion's implied promise. That of excellence that comprise:

❶ Consistency, ❷ Continuity, ❸ Reliability, ❹ Punctuality, ❺ Follow Up, ❻ Follow Through, ❼ Cooperation, ❽ Collaboration, ❾ Commitment, and ❿ Completion.

Some Sample Assignment Ideas

How I'll Handle & Use What I Just Read

❶ _____.

❷ _____.

❸ _____.

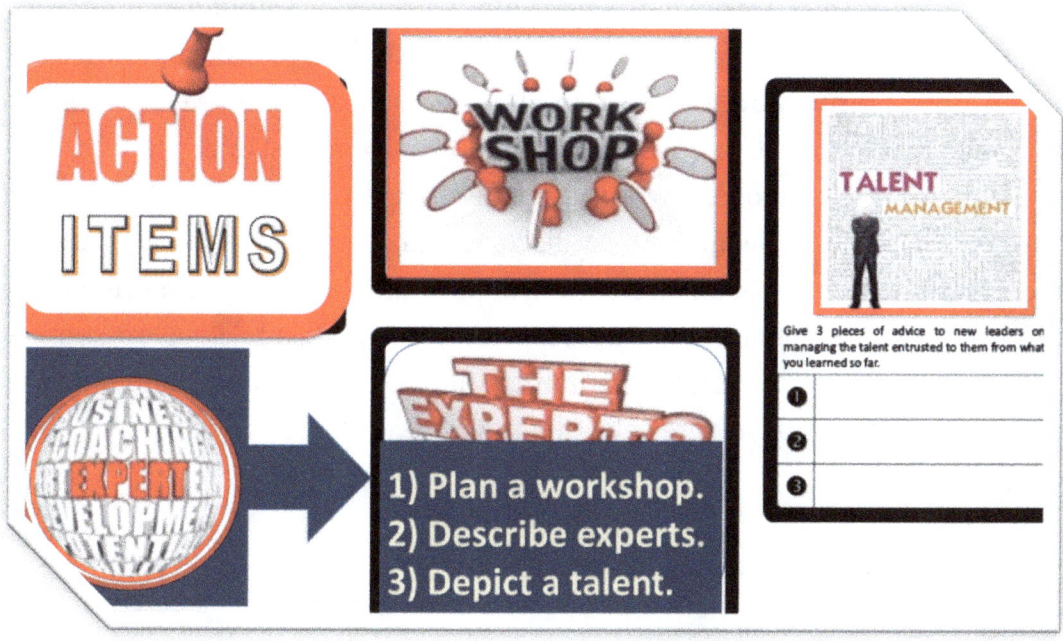

Empowering & Authorizing Your Leaders Responsibly

There are a number of factors and criteria associated with appointing someone to a leadership post. Here I want to summarize some of them to give you cues and clues you can use to evaluate your own leadership choices and the candidacy criteria. If you are newly appointed to leadership, you could appreciate these tips as valuable aids to your adjustment period. The first of the explanations involve:

- Trust
- Accountability

1. **Trust**: It is realistic to accept that trust is a primary part of being appointed to leadership. Those who put promote people have a duty to appoint those that are trustworthy, especially when one considers that one definition of an office is "a position of trust." Take time to ensure those you empower are worthy of the trust that you, and God through you, must put in them.

2. **Accountability**: Although this word is bandied about routinely in different professional circles by modern leaders, the truth is very few of them comprehend fully

what it means. If they did grasp the enormity of the term's application to leadership and its gravity, classes, and practicum would thread its concepts, actions, and manifestations throughout them. Accountability makes one answerable, responsible and liable. These are strong non-negotiable requirements that should be clear to those you decide to put over anybody and anything. Learn how its attributes work in the world of everyday leadership to discover what you should look to see in your appointees. Having a good understanding of its applied meanings assure the ones you want to license or appoint truly possesses them. Be sure to develop some sort of inventory tool that helps you screen and confirm your incoming leaders possess and can perform the reason you are selecting them from others.

CHAPTER 18
MAKING RIGHT SELECTION DECISIONS

Previously, you were told that extensive attention would be given in your guide to "right" appointments done for the right reasons. Here I resume, that discussion. Numerous considerations should influence the mature leader's pre-authorization considerations. Some of them are listed below. Appointers and authorizers should be circumspect about each one of the statements discussed below. They should choose and promote:

1. **The right people:** The only way to determine the right people for what one needs is to clarify what one, as a leader, authorizer, or appointer is charged to do as an entity. This should be clear and settled. From there, the people to engage in the well-defined enterprise or endeavor ought to likewise be clear on how the reason they are appointed looks, acts and works when the human element is attached. Determining and confirming these encompasses knowing people, knowing skills sets and talents, and understanding the spectrum of work and service involved.

Based on this reading, I will relate the following to my leadership role:

Ⓐ _____.
Ⓑ _____.
Ⓒ _____.

2. **The right place:** People placement is important to an organization's success. Properly placing them relies on identifying and classifying defined areas of service to be staffed and the bulk and weight of duties and business to be handled. Comprehending these decide the areas and degrees of specialization required. From there the talents, gifts, capabilities, and competencies for the post can be carried out successfully can be particularized. Leadership is where people are entrusted to serve positions too

important to give to just anyone who interested or available. Pressures, resistance, complexity and such all warn against yoking novices, unprepared or incompatible souls to serious posts. Putting a person with a knack for drawing numbers in a high position, for instance may prove to be counterproductive for you and your organization if they are ill-equipped to manage the numbers they pull. Another example is assigning a shy person to the telephones, for instance, is a misfit that organizations cannot afford no matter how desperately candidates need the work and you need workers. Figure out what skills set go with what tasks and the best department or area to use those you promote as leaders. Take time to correlate the level of knowledge, skill, and the expertise you need with the candidates you consider. Verify they acquired and can perform the criteria set for the position's occupants. Be sure aspirants and nominees promoted to your leadership can undertake your business matters and handle the minutiae awaiting the most qualified people you can obtain to do them. Make every effort to rightly place those you use and stringently prove the ones you place over them.

I will use this information examine my leader promotion motives:

a) _____.
b) _____.
c) _____.

My examination methods will be:

Step I. _____.
Step II. _____.
Step III. _____.

I will put forth the following efforts to increase my adaptability to this wisdom.

Step I. _____.
Step II. _____.
Step III. _____.

3. **The right time:** In life timing is everything and when it comes to putting people in leadership, knowing when they are seasoned enough to succeed and benefit the

organization is paramount. Youthful talent may be impressive, even entertaining, but it is still but a promise that cannot be cashed in on until life has tempered youthful zeal and ripen talents. It takes years to acquire and soundly utilize wisdom, prudence, and experience. Rushing a prospective leader through a training program or preempting one entirely to get what you can out of them may help in the short term but over time it brings grave consequences. Seasoning takes the time it takes and just because a candidate can't see around the corner because of inexperience and lack of exposure, does not mean what you the leader know to be around that corner should be ignored. The time you served to learn to do and think the way you do is valuable. Do not cast aside the instincts you gained from that process under the pressures of a talented eager servant who will be worth more to you in two or three years than they are today. Wait for the precious fruit of the earth and know when and how long to wait for it to be ready for your use. Avoid consuming unripe fruit as a stopgap measure to long-standing or not entirely understood issues. Care enough for your organization and its future to train and prove, and at times, prune, your up and coming leaders. Start them out with simple tasks and observe their approaches, initiatives, and actions. Weigh them against the ultimate load of duties they will bear.

This reading, impacted me in the following ways:

Ⓐ _____.

Ⓑ _____.

Ⓒ _____
_____.

After official placement, continue training and trialing your future leaders until their readiness comes up to the scale of demands waiting for them. When what they can do exceeds what you need them to do, they are ready to be placed, and then, only provisionally. Allow new leaders at least eighteen months of acclimation and adaptation before making them permanent. Stand back and monitor how they handle your promotion and watch how the promotion reacts to them. Keep notes, meet with them regularly, instruct and correct without hesitation. After all, they are your future asset and you want to ensure you set them up for success and not a failure. What hasty promotions inevitably do. Promotees employed before their time stumble, err and frustrate those around them. They lack the disciplines and instincts for what they were appointed to do, despite having the greatest talents and ingenuity for it. What the mind can learn, and the emotions can withstand are often decades apart from each other. Astute appointers should recognize and be governed by this truth.

Overwhelmingness can over saturate the emotions and they, in due course will gradually degrade new appointees' abilities. Young leaders may not realize this is happening until they fizzle out, so to speak. To offset what they can only feel happening, newcomers to leadership turn to crutches to continue functioning. Struggling neophytes typically brace their falls with substance abuse, reckless indulgences, deviancy, escape or avoidance, and other unhealthy or useless copers. At first, they lean on them to treat the performance decline inexperience imposed upon them. Later, they increase their copers to hide theirs out of control spiral. By the time their appointers realize something is wrong a multitude of consequences have long since been in effect; their cost being the last outcome to surface. Ashamed, and probably debilitated by the long slide downhill young untried leaders panicked and depleted admit more time before promotion could have prevented their calamity. A calamity that involves more than themselves.

My perspective on appointing leaders was changed by this section the following significant ways.:

Ⓐ _____.

Ⓑ _____.

Ⓒ _____

_____.

4. **The right reasons:** Motives are important when it comes to choosing people to serve as leaders. Appointers should examine their own motivations for choosing one person over another as diligently as they examine the capabilities of their candidates. Knowing why a particular person appeals to you as a leader and why another raises negative emotions is beneficial. This is true even if the reasons have nothing to do with the job to be done or the abilities needed to do it. Sometimes people who bring friction or tension can be useful to spur the complacent in the group on to diligences they would otherwise evade. So do not be put off by someone who is highly capable

qualified who happens to be emotionally different from you. Notice the word is different, not dysfunctional. That one may be the right one to keep you and your team on track. Moreover, serious positions should not be used as incentive awards if those placed in them are unqualified. Incentives are good but they should equate to what is being offered and balanced by what is to be gained in return. Promoting someone to a higher post just to keep them with you may work for a moment, but it can backfire when they realize how ill-equipped they are for the promotion. Such promotees can end up resenting you for unpleasantly exposing them to discredit because of your compromise. You and your organization deserve to be profited by those you appoint. Be sure to provide yourself as well as your other staff members with heads and hearts, hands and feet that advance and not hinder your vision.

This reading impressed 3 things upon me as a new leader.

a)	
b)	
c)	

Initial procedures I will set up to place my leaders properly will start with:

First.	
Second.	
Third.	

Signs that tell me a leader I put in place is in trouble revolve around:

Step I.	
Step II.	
Step III.	

5. **The right way:** There is a way to do everything that is more expedient to conducive leadership than any other. Leaders should be aware of, how to bring people on board, how to present them to their organizations, and how to stage their success. Casual appointments or authorizing may make a good show, but they can boomerang on you later. Those to be led or affected by a new appointee may resent or resist their

authority simply because they were abruptly put over them. A better approach would be to publicize your decision to bring on a newcomer. Share what the person will bring to your organization and the asset they will be to your team. Schedule a day and time to legitimize their appointment and gather the rest of your workers to witness and participate in it. Avoid sneakily appointing or promoting someone and leaving them to present themselves to your people. The transition period it takes to get accustomed to, or as a new leader can be long and hard under the best conditions. It need not be complicated by impulsive and insensitive insertion of an unfamiliar authority figure.

There is much more to be said on the world of leadership, by now you have here more than enough to get on track and take the lead. Wrap it all up with the next to the last action item.

How I'll Handle & Use What I Just Read
1. _____.
2. _____.
3. _____.

POLISHING YOUR CRITICAL THINKING SKILLS[21]

---

[21] Refer to or review God is a Thinker Handout.

Section End Reading Interaction Project

REINFORCE IT	THINK IT	RECOGNIZE IT	DISCUSS IT	USE IT	TEACH IT
The information you just read contained several wisdoms that you should reinforce and apply in your Leadership Education Classes. Think on them and apply what you just read to newcomer transition to leadership's world and ways.	Produce 3 ways interested and critical people should (could) think about what you just read. Add to your response how you will answer predictable questions that might arise from them.	Denote 3 signs people familiar with and new to leadership in general as portrayed or discussed in your reading view of it would showcase quality leadership as you are learning it now, just read. Illustrate their examples.	Exchange ideas with your group, peers, and colleagues on how those entering or served by this information can settle and thrive in their new leadership roles. Provide at least 5 doable ways they can do so and specific outcomes to note.	Develop 5 ways the material you just read could be used by incoming and experienced leaders coupled with the best environment each one could be used effectively to stabilize new leaders and as a result their organizations.	Draft 3 ways to use the material in this section to orientate new leaders to the world of leadership. Focus your responses on "Ministry Must Change: Entering Leadership Changes You; and New Leader Shocks and Upsets.

Engaging Section Read Wisdom

1. Identify and profile two groups that would best react to your responses based on your readings.
2. Outline how you will approach your most compatible groups' with your responses as a new leader.
3. Depict the way you will present your responses to your most compatible groups using the HK5's.
4. Anticipate the ten main objections you are likely to encounter as a new leader.
5. List your answers to your most compatible groups' objections using what you learned.
6. Design a welcome to the world of leadership plan to expedite your acceptance as a new leader.
7. Project ways you will settle and grow as a new comer to your organization's leadership team.

Training Praxes HK5's
- How to think it
- How to act on it
- How to share it.
- How to build on it
- How to sustain what is built.

Fun Activity: Reviewing Your Journey

Take a moment and have some fun completing your New Leader Transition Journal. Fill it in based on what you now know about entering the world of leadership.

INDEX

accountability, 17, 121
acronym r.o.a.d.w.a.y., 17
acting on what you read, 24
actionizers, and actionables, 44
activating your consciousness, 5, 19
adaptation, 11, 110, 114, 115, 125
adaptive changes, 7, 115
affirmation, 104
anticipate and prepare, 58
the assessment process, 87
attend, 24
attitude and conduct, 106
authority, 84
awakened latent leadership talents, 7
awakened leadership talents, 96
be different, become exceptional, 103
behavior, 25
benefits their entity's, 99
certification, 25
checkups, 116
codes, 25
commands, 65, 117
commands attached to work ethic, 119
community, 101
conduct, 25
constructors and

expanders, 51
criticizing, 84
currency, 101, 104, 105
decision-making skills, 106
downtime, 71, 72
duties, 23, 25
earning trust, 7, 110
emotional infrastructure, 117
emotional self, 116
examine yourself regularly, 99
exceptional, 7
expectations, 84, 90
expectations, 84
familiarizing yourself, 5, 26
family always comes first" rule, 62
family and friends, 62
family first, really, 54
first responses to your rise, 35
functioning effectively in your new position, 82
guardians, 97
guardianship guidance, 7, 111
guidelines, 25
guides & gains, 10
hedge, 97
hostility and disappointment have

short self lives, 69
how we got here, 36
human capital 'c' suite, 93
human instincts, 93
idiosyncrasies, 110
ill-equipped for promotion, 127
immersive training, 9
inborn and inbred assets, 93
incompetence, 118
in-service, 24
installed, 31
instructants, 10
instruction and guidance map, 9
intiatives, 99
inventory, 16, 116, 122
kingdom, 31
leaders are innate teachers, 97
leaders are teachers, 97
leadership appointers, 38
leadership demands, 14, 16, 17, 18, 20, 26, 31, 32, 34, 55, 56, 59, 64, 80, 82, 86, 89, 91, 109, 115, 117, 125
leadership goals, 107
leadership modes, 107
leadership proving, 5, 38
leadership role, 35, 83
leadership strengtheners, 5, 23
leadership transition, 75,

88
leadership's functions and dutifulness, 27
leadership's r.o.b.e.'s of delegation, 44
manifestation, 91
mature leader's, 123
mediocrity, 109
minister, 31
ministry's new day, 36
misguided new leaders, 64
more than mechanics, 7, 97
more than paperwork, 6, 78
neglect, 34, 62, 99, 118, 119
objectives, 12
observable outcomes, 13
official appointment, 108
on the matter of family, 58
ordination, 31
orientation, 25
people builders, 106
people demolishers, 106
people dislike change, 34
people-insight, 93
perception of life, 99
policy, 25
positivity, 104, 105
pre-authorization considerations, 123
preconditioned thoughts and emotions, 64
prime your family for

your leadership, 55
procedures, 25
professional changes, 83
promotion, 31, 80, 82, 88, 90, 91, 108
promotion creates a new life, 31
protect your organization, 98
protocol, 98
public appearance, 31
rationale, 12
renovation of the broken, 106
requisite leadership changes, 7, 102
responsibilities, 25
responsive thinking, 42
right" appointments, 123
saboteur of your promotion, 70
safety and security, 107
saul and David's leadership appointment, 39
self-celebratory leader, 65
self-deprecating leader, 6, 66
shocks & wake-ups, 7, 90
sound judgment, 106
stunners, 107
supervisor, 89
supplement goal, 12
supplement interactions,

11
t.r.a.c.k. acronyms, 42
takeaways, 14
tendencies and reflexes, 116
the six a's, 16
the wisdom pack, 7, 94
threats, 108
training, 24
triple v, 116, 117, 119
triple v competence, 116, 119
trip-ups, 116
trust, 121
tutorial overview, 10
underlying attitudes and reactions to your leadership, 60
an unfamiliar authority figure, 128
unmanageables, 83
unveiling, 91
vain imaginations, 107
ventures, 107
visualizing, 86
vocabulary, 14
volitional tenacity, 117
wonder worker, 89
your leadership adjustment, 5, 20

Created 2014 ©, Revised 2019 ©
Dr. Paula A. Price, PhD
All Rights Reserved

www.ingramcontent.com/pod-product-compliance
Lightning Source LLC
Chambersburg PA
CBHW080912170426
43201CB00017B/2306